M

NOTES ON ANDRÉ GIDE

ROGER MARTIN DU GARD

NOTES ON

André Gide

TRANSLATION AND FOREWORD

BY JOHN RUSSELL

HELEN MARX BOOKS

NEW YORK

First published as *Notes sur André Gide, 1913–1951*
by Roger Martin du Gard. Gallimard, Paris, 1951.

Also published in 1953 by Andre Deutsch Limited.
This edition copyright © 2005 by Helen Marx Books.

ISBN 1-885586-31-0 LCCN 2004106079

FRONTISPIECE: *André Gide*, circa 1910–1920.
Photograph. © Hulton-Deutsch Collection / Corbis.

*No man is the same
as the total of his appearances*

PAUL VALÉRY

This book is not long, and everything in it is stylishly put and absolutely to the point. André Gide was for many years a controversial figure not only in French literature but also in French life. To a large public of Left Bank literati, he was the gifted and influential writer who had "come out" as a homosexual. To a less enlightened public, he was iniquitous.

One of the book's merits is that it gives equal time to the not-often-mentioned Madame André Gide. If Madame Gide was always delighted to see Roger Martin du Gard, and if he was touched and moved to see her, it was because he was a distinguished writer in his own right who had known from the outset that her marriage to Gide—or, for that matter, anyone's marriage to Gide—was misconceived.

Roger Martin du Gard noticed that beneath the impeccable courtesies she and Gide showed to one another in private was "an absence of anything approaching the normal familiarity of marriage" and that beneath it all lay "an impenetrable coldness." But then he knew that some time before their marriage

Gide had written to his future wife, "I do not desire you. Your body is an embarrassment to me, and I have always been horrified by physical possession." He was also to find out that she had burnt all of Gide's letters, the better to detach herself from him. As he said later, "I was what I was. She was what she was. We both suffered bitterly, in consequence. It could not have been otherwise."

"Why did they bother?" is the commonsense reply to those remarks. But common sense played no part in the relationships in question. What counted was Gide's reputation, which at the time was overwhelming. This was important not only to Gide and his many distinguished admirers but also to the international standing of recent French literature. André Gide was not "a great writer" in the sense that Proust was a great writer, but for many readers he was an irresistible writer.

Roger Martin du Gard knew that Gide was forever assembling and manipulating the raw material of his upcoming books. As he said, "Gide is a man of letters, from morning till night. Even in love, even when making love." And when he returned home from distant travels, Gide did not really want to talk about what he had seen and (still less) what he had done. He wanted to hear the latest news from the literary Left

Bank: who was in, and who was out, and who was on the way up.

The friends of André Gide were not a secret society, as many people believed, but they were a private society that did not wish to be enlarged. If two of its members met in mixed company, they did not bandy the favored name. They would draw apart from the others and murmur, "What news of . . . the rue Vaneau?" If Gide dropped some of his old friends, his loyal adherents would put a good face on it and say (as did Roger Martin du Gard) that he was "doing what we should all do, from time to time— reviewing his treaties of alliance."

As this indispensable book makes clear, Gide was on the job, eighteen if not twenty-four hours a day. This is not to say that he was always writing, but he was continually making himself ready to write. Even when he was making love, as Roger Martin du Gard remarked, he was often taking mental notes. But that is true of just about every painter, every poet, and every dramatist of stature.

Theirs is a way of life in which the day-to-day may be put aside at any moment. But the day-to-day also has its magical surprises. Roger Martin du Gard describes how he was once reading his most recent work to Gide while they were sitting out of doors overlooking a little harbour. Gide was his courteous self, never missing a word.

But suddenly two personable young men appeared below and began larking around. Gide noticed them and at once took up his spectacles. Without missing a word of what his friend was saying, he forthwith kept tabs on the two young men. His opinions, when expressed, were as valid and as generous as ever. But he wasn't going to miss the impromptu cabaret. Nor was he expected to.

Gide was not "of a piece." He made and remade himself, throughout his life. And that's how we like to remember him.

JOHN RUSSELL

NOTES ON ANDRÉ GIDE

NOVEMBER 1913

At last I have met André Gide!

Last Sunday I was invited to the *Nouvelle Revue Française* before dinner. It was their monthly reception for contributors and friends.

In the shop in the rue Madame, I found about a dozen young men, grouped round Gaston Gallimard and Jean Schlumberger (the author of *L'Inquiète Paternité*). On the counter, between the accountant's ledgers and the typewriter, were some cups, none of them matching, and a plateful of dry buns. The editorial secretary, a tall, thin, and very young man with a graceful awkwardness of manner, had a smile for us all as he handed round the tea. We might have been in a boys' club. His name is Jacques Rivière. (Copeau is still nominally in charge of the magazine; but since the Vieux-Colombier opened, not long ago, he has no time for anything but his theatre). I had already met Jean Schlumberger. As he moved from one to another of us there was a well-mannered coolness about him: even he himself seemed intimidated by it, and it was touching to see how he tried to transform it into an appearance of smiling good-nature.... My *Jean Barois* has just come out, and I was both flattered and embarrassed by the curiosity with which everyone crowded round to speak to me about it. They all said that it was a remarkable book; but I soon had the feeling that not one of them—not even Gaston, perhaps?—had read it, really read it, from cover to cover.

In the middle of the next room I found a hilarious, uproarious Bluebeard in a state of demoniac excitement. It was Henri Ghéon: two flaring eyes in a radiant face; a beard—square, dark, short and thick; florid cheeks; a gleaming cranium. As he turned towards me there was tenderness and cruelty and great good spirits in his glance. He overwhelmed me with exaggerated compliments. He spluttered and gesticulated as he talked, and punctuated every conversation with a loud whinnying: you feel that he is drunk, perpetually drunk, with the fact of being alive.

I moved on. Now it was Paul Fargue who pinned me against the window. A face made into a perfect egg-shape by the tall, bulging, disgarnished forehead and the pointed end of his beard. Almond eyes, wrinkled eyelids, a caressing glance which, though seemingly distracted, misses nothing. A strange mixture of quivering sensuality and oriental impassivity. As he talked, with a cigarette planted square in the middle of his face, there was no more than the barest perceptible parting of his delicately-pursed lips. The voice is soft, and coaxes. He listens to himself, as if he were dictating an article and savouring, as a connoisseur, each passing phrase. He claimed to have devoured my *Barois* in a single night: he described himself—not without satisfaction—smoking, now lying flat, now hoisting himself upon one elbow, in the intimate circle of the lamplight; and it seemed as if the soft, rose-pink light, the warm bed, the silence of the night, the intoxication of tobacco and the interest of my novel had fused in a single voluptuous memory.

The door is pushed ajar. A man sidles into the shop, as a down-and-out slips into the warmth of a church. His eyes are hidden behind the brim of a battered old hat; an enveloping cloak hangs down from his shoulders. He looks like an old, half-starved, out-of-work actor; or like one of those bohemian wrecks who end up in a doss-house when their luck's right out; or else like one of those habitués of the Bibliothèque Nationale, professional copyists with their dubious collars and cuffs, who fall asleep on their folios in the middle of the day after lunching off a *croissant*. Or an unfrocked priest, perhaps? An unfrocked priest with a bad conscience? Gautier accused Renan of having kept his 'parsonical look'. . . . But they all go to greet him; evidently he has something to do with the magazine. He takes off his hat and his cloak; his shapeless, outworn travelling-suit doesn't seem to belong to his awkward limbs; his detachable collar, frayed and hanging loose, reveals a neck like that of some elderly bird; the hair recedes from the forehead and is beginning to turn grey; tufty above the coat-collar, it looks drab, as if it were dead at the roots. The Mongol mask, in which the oblique ridges of the brow predominate, is flawed by warts. The features are emphatic, but flaccid; the complexion is greyish, the cheeks hollow and ill-shaven; the line of the thin-set lips is sinuous and elastic; there is no candour in the eyes, as they hover beneath the eyelids, and with the momentary flashing glance there goes a smile that is almost a grimace: a smile at once childlike and sly, at once timid and rehearsed.

Schlumberger brings him over to me. I am dumbfounded: it is André Gide. . . .

The three of us exchange a few conventional phrases. Gide seems dreadfully embarrassed, and of course this makes my own shyness the more acute. After a few moments Schlumberger leaves us together. Gide hesitates, goes and gets his cloak, turns quickly towards me, hesitates again, and then—with a furtive glance to left and to right, and that air of exaggerated

mystery with which an inexperienced actor signals to
his audience that he is about to do someone down—
he draws me into the empty back room of the shop,
among the stacks of books and the bales of paper. And
there, not looking me in the eye, squatting on a pair of
library steps, and leaning forward in the attitude of a
gargoyle, he murmurs a few amiable words to me in a
tone of pretentious embarrassment. What does he say?
That he had been interested to read my book? No: that
he had been compelled, in self-defence, to take my
enormous manuscript to the country, this last summer;
that he had been first bored, and then later surprised,
by what he read; that he had been 'very curious indeed' to meet the author; and that he was astonished
to find that I was barely more than thirty.... I say little or nothing in reply. And then suddenly he looks
up, puts one elbow on his knee, rests his chin on his
hand (closed, but not clenched), looks at me, and begins to talk quite freely. The voice flows easily and naturally; it has an admirable timbre—deep, warm, sol-
emn. A voice that coaxes and whispers, a voice made
for confidences, with the subtlest modulations, and just
occasionally an abrupt heightening of tone to make
way for a rare epithet or an original, meaningful turn
of phrase. At such moments he seems to launch the
word in triumph upon the air, to allow it its full reso-
nance—much as one lifts a diapason to allow it its

maximum vibration.* I don't know what to think, let alone what to say ... The ideas which he develops and defines in this burst of improvisation are completely new to me, alike in substance and in form. Their iridescence dazzles me. Never, in conversation, has anybody given me such an impression of natural power, of *genius*. ...

Perhaps all that brilliance would be insupportable if I could detect in it the element of artifice; but Gide seems true to himself even in his preciosities and his coquetry, and it is with enchantment that I yield to his seduction. What does he look like? I examine him with new eyes. When he came in, I had seen him, but I hadn't looked at him. I disregard the two-days' growth of beard, the unkempt hair, the rumpled collar. How vividly I notice, now, the nobility of the face, instinct with feeling and intelligence, the subtle tenderness of his smile, the musical voice, and the attentive and glowing good nature with which he envelops me! For now he never takes his eyes off my face. Quite palpably, he wants me to respond, to fall in with what he is saying; it is an exchange that he offers, it is an ally that he is after. All this quite overwhelms me. Emboldened by it, I make haste to reply; I should have

*Baudelaire also, according to one of his contemporaries, had 'italics and capitals' in his voice.

liked to describe the ever-remembered day when I discovered his *Nourritures Terrestres*. . . .

But suddenly, with no warning, no change of tone,
without even finishing the phrase he had begun—allowing it, in fact, to peter out in an indistinct murmur,
accompanied by some unintelligible motions of the
head and the most affectionate of smiles—Gide gets
up: lithe, graceful, hasty, awkward—he is all these
things at once. He puts on his hat, throws his flowing
cloak over one shoulder, and vanishes from the shop
without giving his hand to anyone—not even to me.

I wonder if he came just to find out what the author
of *Jean Barois* looks like?

Sainte-Beuve says of Maine de Biran:

'He has from the outset one blessed faculty, which
is the basis of all discovery, all original observation: he
is amazed by what seems simple to the majority of
mankind, and where others are blind, through habit,
to the marvellous complication of the world, his eyes
are open.'*

*Professor Leriche, for whom André Gide had both respect and
admiration, wrote later, of Claude Bernard, that 'the man of genius . . . is the man whose mind fastens upon things which the rest
of us do not notice; and, once established there, he sees what the
rest of us do not see.'

Gide talks of nothing but the composing of his *Memoirs*, of which an extract has appeared in the N.R.F.* He is completely absorbed in them.

'I've hardly reached my adolescence, but I've already come up against some very difficult problems ... One strange thing, my dear Roger—if I could borrow from Christian terminology, if I dared to introduce into my narrative the character of Satan, the whole thing would become miraculously clear—easy to write, easy to understand ... Things have always worked out for me as if the Devil existed and had constantly intervened in my affairs....'†

What drove him to write this autobiography, he says, is the conviction that the story of his first twenty-five years had general implications which far outrun the interest of an individual adventure.

He admits that he always needs—protestant atavism, perhaps?—to justify his conduct by analysis and explanation and enquiry into its hidden motives. Not

---

Si le grain ne meurt.

†In Gide's posthumous *Ainsi soit-il*, there occurs the passage: 'If I believed in the Devil (and I've sometimes pretended to: it's so convenient) I should say that....'

M. Paul Claudel asserts—not altogether seriously—in *Figures et Paraboles* that 'It's only when Goethe is inspired by Mephisto that he has any talent'.

for the satisfaction of proving that he was right to do as he did; but because he claims the right to be as he is; and because, being as he is, he could not behave otherwise than as he does.

He demands of himself, in this effort of recollection, the strictest accuracy:

'I do not wish to alter the smallest detail. I shan't change a single name—nor even the colour of anybody's hair. If my confession is to be worth anything—if it is to have the value which I want it to have—it must be completely truthful. If I am to deserve to be believed, I've got to be able to say: "You see—there's no deception at all. Every factual detail is correct. And the same, exactly the same, is true of all the rest. Improbable as it may seem to you, that is how things are, and that is how I am".'

MARCH 1920

Gide lunches with us.

He complains how difficult it is to organise one's working life in Paris. I second him. I describe how, in the war, when I thought of the various ways in which I might be mutilated, I happened to imagine myself blinded by a shell-burst: and how I saw myself, condemned to perpetual meditation, the exhilarated prisoner of my own concentrated mind, dictating to my wife a series of quite admirable books.... Gide listens

9

with an astonished, wondering attentiveness which my conversation does little to deserve.

A little later, he tells me why:

'Quite by chance you gave me, just now, an idea for the end of the *Oedipus* that I am thinking of writing ... What I should like to do, you see, is to present, at the beginning of the play, an Oedipus triumphant, glorying in his success, a man of action, without a care in the world: a "Goethean" Oedipus. And then, with no change in the *facts* of his situation, but simply by the intervention, and the influence, of a priest, a *Christian* Tiresias, this vainglorious Oedipus is stripped of his entire happiness. A fine subject, don't you think? You see the point: nothing, not one single thing, has altered around him;* but all that had hitherto made him the most assured, the most balanced, the most completely satisfied of monarchs comes suddenly to count for nothing—and simply because the high priest has changed the lighting ... or in other words because the Christian perspective has taken the place of the pagan perspective.... And now I can glimpse the end of my play: the hapless king possessed by one desire, and one only: to escape into blindness from the present—to escape that present which, for him, has been ruined be-

---

*Nothing altered! He learns that he has killed his father, and married his mother, and so on.... Nothing to speak of, I suppose!

1 0

yond repair; to retreat into that night, peopled with
the memory of past happiness, which alone can restore
his optimistic view of the world and his taste for
life. . . .'

★

Gide read me this page of Buffon:

'It may be that by moderation in the passions, and
by sobriety and temperance in one's pleasures, one
may hope to live longer. But even that is very doubt-
ful. Perhaps the body needs to use up all its strength,
to consume all that it can possibly consume, and to
exert itself to the limit of its powers.'

In this connection Montaigne's avowal is worth re-
membering:

'Whenever I have a chance, however small, of en-
joying myself, I grab it.'

OCTOBER 1920

I had an appointment with Gide this morning at the
Villa Montmorency, to hear him read aloud from *Si le
grain* . . . (The sketch for the second part.)

He's left the door ajar. I call to him and his voice
answers from a long way off. All the doors in the house
are open. He comes running, with his manuscript in
his hand. I have the feeling that while he was waiting
for me he wandered alone through one after another

11

of these deserted echoing rooms, like the last man aboard an abandoned liner. The odd, fabulous house where he seems so strangely not at home—where it seems impossible, in fact, that anybody should ever feel at home. . . . He steers me impatiently through the circumvolutions of the staircase, whose preposterous design might have been intended to illustrate a story of Edgar Allan Poe. It's like the staircase of a lighthouse, stuck on to the inside wall of an enormous, terrifyingly empty cage. The successive sections of this staircase are very disconcerting; some of them are like booby-traps, and lead no one knows where: nowhere at all, perhaps. . . . Up on the first floor, I follow Gide along a corridor; through a wide-open door I glimpse a ship's cabin, with the bed unmade. We climb a few more steps. Another corridor, half blocked with suitcases. We go past a rickety folding table, heaped high with papers; a kitchen stool stands against a big radiator. 'That's where I usually work; but you'll be more comfortable along here,' says Gide, as he waves me on. More steps. Eventually we reach a sort of tiny loggia, with windows everywhere, which stands like a lookout post above a dark hall in which I can discern tables, bookcases, armchairs covered with dust-sheets, and piles of books that overflow even on to the floor. In this room—this poop, I should say—two little hard armchairs of dark wood are ready for us.

Gide is already seated, with his manuscript open in front of him on a little table wedged into the embrasure of the window. Outside, I can see roofs, and the top of a cedar tree. The light falls on Gide's fine head. His whole face is alive with pleasure. He puts on the tortoiseshell spectacles (which sit now above, now below, the wart on his nose, according to whether it is me or the manuscript that he is looking at). Without preamble, with gluttonous haste, in fact, he begins to read. (The journey to Biskra, with Jean-Paul Laurens.) He is clearly deeply moved by the reading; his mouth and hands are shaking.

There follows a long and candid discussion. I ask him to repeat certain passages, and I point out to him that throughout the narrative there is a note of implied reprobation, orthodox in tone and protestant, no doubt, in origin.

'Good heavens,' he says, in a disturbed voice. 'The eternal drama of my life. . . . You realise, don't you, my dear Roger, that all that is for my wife? It was with her ever-present in my mind that I wrote it.'

In point of fact this confession, which he meant to be complete, with nothing held back, seems to me still rather cautious, full of points at which he has shut down, or covered up, or simply refused to come out. Faced with certain avowals, he seems to withdraw in spite of himself. I tell him so. He agrees at once, with a touching readiness, a sort of delight and exaltation in accusing himself:

'Yes, yes ... I see just what you mean.... What you tell me is exactly what I think myself.... All in all, I *did* cheat a little, without wanting to ... I shirked the real heart of the matter. And the rest goes for nothing, doesn't it, if the heart of the matter has been left out....'★

He suddenly decides not to stay in Paris, but to go as soon as possible to Cuverville, to be more alone with himself and get back to his work. He'll go today, this instant....

I go with him in the taxi to Saint-Lazare. He doesn't say a word all the way. But just as we get there he leans towards me:

'Forgive me for not talking ... but what we've just

★From Gide's *Journal*: *October 8th 1920*. R.M.G.... tells me that he is deeply disappointed: I've evaded the real subject: from fear, or modesty, or regard for the public, I've not dared to say anything that is really intimate. I've only succeeded in arousing people's curiosity.

And yet I feel that I've put down all that I can remember of my childhood, and with the greatest possible indiscretion....

November 1st. Struggling with the intermediary chapters of my *Memoirs*, which are meant to go in between the book as it was printed, and the part that I wrote this summer. (The journey in Algeria with Paul A. Laurens.) I should like these new chapters to satisfy the exigences of R.M.G.

said is so important, my dear Roger! I can already see exactly what has to be altered. . . . I couldn't think of anything else any more!'

A long visit from Gide.

I remind him of what he said about me—before he knew me—in the summer of 1913 when he advised the NRF to publish *Jean Barois*: 'He may not be an artist, but he's a thoroughly good fellow.'

'Don't distress yourself about not being an *artist*,' he says, with a laugh. 'There's much too much of the artist about the rest of us. Don't be like Charles-Louis Philippe. That's a case I saw at close quarters: a pathetic case. . . . He had real creative power. Contact with us was fatal to him . . . he was constantly restraining, distorting, mutilating himself in order to become more of an *artist*; and he ruined his gift. . . . Remember that the great creative geniuses never started from a preconceived theory of art; they attained to art by their own act of creation, without having wanted to do it, without knowing it; that's why their art was personal to themselves; that's why it was new.'

The conversation turns upon the novel, the novelist, and the gift of observation.

'I must admit that it's only very recently that my eyes were opened to life, and to other people. . . . In fact

I can say that never, until I was forty, did I care to notice what was going on around me. The problem of religion and the problem of sex absorbed me completely; they seemed to me insoluble, but I could find nothing else that was worthy of attention. I lived like a blind man....'

1920

Copeau said to me: 'André lacks a gift that is essential to the true novelist; he doesn't know how to stand boredom. The moment anyone ceases to stimulate him, he loses all interest. It's the same with the characters in his books: he usually begins to lose interest in them towards the hundred-and-fiftieth page; and so he rounds the story off anyhow, the quicker the better, like a schoolboy with an imposition.'*

1920

I told him that if I had to choose one of his books to take away, by itself, to a desert island, my choice would fall upon *Saül*. He seemed surprised. Then, with a smile:

*That is what happened with the *Faux-Monnayeurs*. Gide planned to write several more chapters before completing the book; but he had lost momentum. It was then that he hit on the famous little phrase: 'I am very interested to get to know Caloub.' It seemed to him, as he said, such a suggestive 'last line' that he at once decided to stop there—delighted to be rid of the book!

'Do you know that that play was nearly put on at the Théâtre Antoine? He very much wanted to produce it. He said to me—on the only occasion I met him, by the way—"Monsieur Gide, your *Saül* is a very good play! If my next production is a success, I shall have enough money, and I shall at once put your play into rehearsal." The next production was Brieux's *Résultat des Courses*. My heart was in my mouth as I hurried to the first performance. At first I tried to persuade myself that it was excellent—such was my anxiety that it should succeed. But with the second act I had to give in to the facts: it was an execrable play, a complete failure! I was done for, and I went out before the third act.... And that's how my *Saül* was the victim of Brieux's *Résultat des Courses....*'

Sainte-Beuve says of Goethe:

'He was inquisitive—insistently, anxiously so—but without ever risking himself entirely.'

I point out that he has just contradicted himself. He replies with a smile:

'You remember what Stendhal said: "I have a double self: a good way of not making mistakes...."'

Was it meant quite as a joke?

Gide has come to spend three days with me in my little retreat at Clermont. I read to him the *Cahier Gris*
and half the *Penitencier.*

(An immediate note of an amusing misunder-
standing.

On one of my first visits to his villa at Auteuil, my
curiosity was attracted by a large and much-worn volume which occupied a prominent place on a table not
far from my chair. Naturally I looked at the title:
P. Boissière, *Dictionnaire Analogique.* 'Aha!' I said to myself, 'perhaps this is the secret of Gide's vocabulary and
the source of his felicities? I too must have a Boissière!'
The hunt was up at once. But the book is old, out of
print, impossible to find. I put my booksellers on the
alert. Eventually they dug up a copy—ill-bound,
falling to pieces, wickedly expensive. I paid up without a murmur, and set myself to make good use of it.

But when he arrives at Clermont Gide goes through
my books. 'Ah,' he says, 'you've got that compilation
of Boissière's? What d'you make of it?' 'Oh, it's in-
comparable!' 'Really? I bought one once, but I've
never opened it. I've never been able to use such
things....')

★

Three days alone together—reading aloud, talking
interminably. (When he gives me advice about my

books, he never, so to say, pulls the blankets over to his side; he puts himself in my position, and the object of his injunctions is to make me *be myself* in the greatest possible degree. Faced with a page that doesn't come off, he never says: 'This is what I should have done,' but: 'This is what you would have done yourself if you'd been on your best form.')★

He too would like to write a long and elaborate novel, packed with incident. He tells me the subject: a group of semi-delinquent children falls in by chance with a gang of coiners; to prove themselves true members of the gang, they are driven to offer a pledge—in other words, to commit an act of illegality by which they are irreparably compromised.

His scheme is still in its earliest stages. But, in speaking about it, he made me realise how absolutely different—how opposite, in fact—are our ways of looking at the novel-form. (I feel that my view is still very elementary. What I call objectivity, fidelity to the real, simplicity of composition and texture—all these may merely be forms of indigence.)

To make himself doubly clear, he takes a clean sheet of paper and draws a horizontal line straight across it. Then, taking my pocket torch, he shines the circle of

★Gide's *Journal: December 22nd 1920.* Spent two days at Clermont.... Uninterrupted conversations—of the greatest profit, I think, to both of us....

light along the pencilled line, from one end to the other. 'There you have your *Barois* and your *Thibault.* . . . You imagine the biography of your main character, or the fortunes of your family, and you shine your light upon the subject, year by year, as best you can. . . . But now this is how I set about the *Faux-monnayeurs.* . . .' He turns the page over, traces a big semi-circle upon it, puts the torch in the middle, and revolves it in such a way that the light follows the semi-circular line while the torch itself never leaves the centre of the page. 'D'you see, my dear Roger? These are two different aesthetic systems. You set out your facts, like a historian, in chronological order. Your book is like a panorama that unrolls itself before the reader. You never describe the past through the intermediary of the present, or through the intermediary of a character who had no part in the incident. You never show us things seen from the side, or from a surprising or anachronistic point of view. Everything, in your novels, is bathed in the same clear, direct, unsurprising light. You deprive yourself, in fact, of some of your most valuable resources. . . .⋆ Think of Rembrandt—

⋆This subject often recurred in our conversations. I read in Gide's *Journal* for *January 3rd 1922*: 'Lunched with R.M.G. at his home. As soon as the meal was over I began to criticise his novel— or rather, more generally, his way of writing it—and this led us in very deep. He was passionately concerned with the subject, and

of his sudden highlights, and the secret depths of his shadow. Lighting is a subtle science in itself: there's a whole art in the infinite variety of it.'

'An art? Or an artifice?'

'Just as you like, my dear Roger. You are true to your own nature. You are on the side of Tolstoy. I am—or I'd like to be—on the side of Dostoevsky. Mark you, I have a profound admiration for Tolstoy. As a *witness*, he's marvellous. But I must own that that's not enough for me. His researches always bear upon what is most general—I might almost say: what is most human—in his characters: on what, in each of us, is common to us all. He shows me, more or less, what I know already; what I could have found out for myself, with a little application. His work has almost no surprises for me.....* Dostoevsky, on the other hand,

---

seemed to wish to acquire certain qualities (the mysterious, the shadowed, and the strange) which are the antithesis of his own character. They are all qualities which are given only to those artists who have flirted with the Devil. And for more than a solid hour, we talked of the *indirect presentation* of events.'

*Gide's *Journal: October 2nd 1936*. In all psychological questions Roger eliminates not only the exceptional, but even the minority. And he even does this—in fact he does it above all—when he is writing his novels. This explains a certain 'banalisation' which marks his characters. He never stops asking: 'What is it that *most usually* happens, in a case of this sort?' The 'one-in-a-thousand'

amazes me all the time! He's always revealing something new, something unexpected, something I've never seen before!'

After a few moments' reflection, he added:

'There's Ibsen, too, by the way. His characters are as true as Tolstoy's; and no less individual, quite often, no less unexpected, than Dostoevsky's....'

APRIL 1921

Gide arrived in the late afternoon and dined with us.

(There are certain days on which he seems keyed-up from the moment he comes in; from the radiant gravity of his manner we know that it is he who will lead the conversation, and that we have only to abandon ourselves. He will run through twenty subjects before arriving at the one which haunts him on that particular day. For there is always a *subject for the day*: one which obsesses him, and one to which all others lead him ineluctably back: he will circle round it for a long time, with many a mysterious shake of the head, as if he were playing at hide-and-seek with himself:

---

doesn't hold his attention; or, if it does, it's merely to relate the case to some great general law. (He's perfectly right, in that, of course.) But it is in the search for that general law that I, on the contrary, concern myself with the exceptions. It is they who claim my vigilant attention, and I find great instruction in them.

but eventually he will pounce upon it. It may be at the last possible moment, when his hand is on the handle of the door; but he will come back, and sit down, and at last he will say what is really on his mind—what is, in fact, the only reason for his visit!)

What is indescribable is the *tone* of this sort of evening, the unexpected twists and turns of the talk. I shall note only what he said about heredity:

'I have every reason to suppose that I am the first homosexual in my family. Search as I may among my ancestors I can find nobody who was not a stiff, inhibited Protestant; if ever they had inclinations of that kind, they fought against them. They suppressed them. Yes, that's how it was! And I am their victim. . . . People don't deny their most natural impulses for many generations with impunity. The moment comes when Nature gets the better of them. It is through me, if I may so put it, that she revenges herself upon them and their severities ... I am paying for them. I am their punishment. . . .'

When I asked a question, he answered quite confidently:

'No, I'm quite sure that my particular tastes could not be inherited: they are acquired traits, which cannot be transmitted. I am as I am because education and environment combined to run counter to my true instincts. . . . As I see it, I must have inherited quite

unusually strong sexual instincts which had been re-
strained and deliberately repressed by generation after
generation of ascetics, so that they press upon *me*, as it
were, with redoubled force. . . .'

★

'Disorderly conduct sharpens the mind and falsifies the
judgment.' BONALD

JANUARY 1922

Gide had met Rathenau at the Maerisch's, in Luxem-
burg. The German minister was in Paris on a mission
and Gide went to see him.

Rathenau's views were of the darkest:

'Things are moving so fast, Monsieur Gide, that
even the most pessimistic forecasts will be realised
much sooner than people think. Henceforward we are
at the mercy of the most insignificant incident. It may
break out in Poland, in Yugoslavia, anywhere. . . .
France bears a heavy responsibility for this! Her igno-
rance of all these new problems dumbfounds me. Your
service estimates alone absorb half the national Bud-
get. Where will that lead you? To bankruptcy? Or rev-
olution? Or war? Europe is heading for the abyss.
There's no way of stopping that—and if there were,
Monsieur Gide, it might be undesirable to attempt it.

The abscess has formed: and it has to be lanced, yet once again.'

Rathenau also said:

'The great factor of the future is that vast, unthinking, unfeeling American people. . . . It is they who, with closed eyes, will impose their decision upon the Old World. . . .'

MARCH 1922

Gide confides to me that he 'absolutely must' publish *Si le grain ne meurt* and *Corydon* without further delay.

I do my best, I do all I can think of, to dissuade him:

'I should be the last to restrain you, if I had any doubt at all of the uselessness, the pathetic uselessness, of the scandal. And a scandal there will inevitably be: one which will put decisive weapons in the hands of your enemies—who are many. It will cut you off from two-thirds of your friends—those, I mean, who accept your private life so long as it is discreet, so long as the veil is not lifted, so long as you keep up appearances; but on the day you make public and cynical avowal of your habits, they will have to take sides; and they will take sides against you. The whole thing is absurd. . . . You're going to surround yourself with an atmosphere of indignation, contempt, and calumny. I know you: you will suffer cruelly as a consequence.

And this is what really makes me despair: for nothing could be more harmful to the full and final expansion of your gifts. . . .'

He watches me with the greatest affection while I say all this; but at the end he shakes his head, gently but stubbornly:

'No, I can't bear to wait any more . . . I have to yield to this overriding interior necessity. Understand me, Roger. I must, I absolutely *must* disperse the cloud of lies which has sheltered me since my youth, since my childhood in fact. . . . I'm stifling behind it!'

He has always been haunted by the tragic destiny of Oscar Wilde. It's quite possible that he believes he has a supreme duty, a higher mission, to fulfil; and that what he is yielding to at this moment is a nostalgic summons to martyrdom. Copeau thinks so; and so, perhaps, may others.

I myself think that it results from his intoxication with Russia: for months he has been living in daily intimacy with Dostoevsky, while preparing his lectures for the Vieux-Colombier. The idea of public confession is infectious; like the hero of a Russian novel, Gide is burning to affront Society and invite its punishment; outrage, opprobrium, the pillory—those are the things to which he aspires. . . . He has such a strange inspired smile when he disposes of my objections! When he thinks of being misunderstood, shunned and despised—the expiatory victim of a sublime sincerity—I believe he feels enlarged and exalted. (For I can sense, in this adventure, some half-formed longing for *expiation*; a new mark, in fact, of those moral reflexes which he has inherited from his puritan ancestors; it is the extension, I would say, of his latent sense of sin—not that he knows of its existence; he would certainly deny it—but I have often noticed the vestiges of it in his behaviour: above all, for instance, in his perpetual wish to explain and defend himself—to *justify* himself, in fact. For it is to that that this great rebel, who believes himself completely emancipated, has hitherto devoted, on his own admission, the best part of his intelligence, and of his gifts.*

*Quite apart from this, he thinks this a propitious moment. Privately, he believes that the hour has come to strike a great blow, so that homosexuality may at last demand for itself a free place in the sun. Himself attentive to the most trifling of indications, he is persuaded that public opinion on this subject has been profoundly modified; and that— —notably under the influence of Freud—sexual questions have acquired a topical interest; that taboos have been abolished; and that we are moving rapidly towards the greatest liberty of conduct.

But all this is true only in appearance. Gide mistakes the wish for the reality. He sees a fundamental acceptance, a general moral re-orientation, in what is no more than one of the varied manifestations of a general, superficial, and temporary relaxation. The upheavals of the war, and the fatigue and confusion of the public mind, are responsible. People react more feebly, are less readily

It is a waste of my time to try to convince him. He will publish his *Corydon*; he will publish *Si le grain de meurt*. In his present exalted state of mind he is ready to sacrifice everything—his good name, his growing reputation as a writer, his peace of mind: and even Emmanuèle's peace of mind.... Has he the right to do this? That is another question .... He is inaccessible to reason. He follows what he calls the natural incline of his career; the more disproportionate the sacrifice, the more intoxicating his own mystical enjoyment....

(And we mustn't forget that Gide has never had the patience to keep a completed manuscript in his drawer for very long.)

---

indignant, are generally less aggressive. All that is true. But the fact that certain moral principles are less vigorously defended does not mean that they are weaker at the roots. We may seem less strict, in such matters, in France; there may be greater freedom of expression in print; the police may be less rigorous; conventional people may be less prudish. But essentially nothing—nothing at all—has changed—neither in the repressions of the law, nor in the attitude of the great majority of our contemporaries. Perhaps this will soon become clear.... The homosexuals may benefit, for the time being, from a tolerance in which apathy now plays a larger part; but in point of fact homosexuality remains subject to the same penalties as before. And in the eyes, not only of most moralists, but of the immense majority of French people, it carries with it the same stigmas, and the same condemnation: a condemnation from which there is no appeal.

★

'Never hesitate to do that which will rid you of half your supporters and triple the affection of those who remain.' PAUL VALÉRY: *Regards sur le monde actuel*

★

'The particular quality of Dostoevsky's work is that he never allows the passions to work themselves out in feeling and action alone; they have to come to terms with Thought; they have to ratiocinate, to invent a justification for themselves, and to construct a theory by which the entire Universe is modelled upon them alone.' MICHEL ARNAUD (M. DROUIN): *N.R.F.* August 1923

★

From an article by Gilliard on Baudelaire (in *Ecrits Nouveaux*, July 1921).

'... a man who was compelled to witness, in his works, to the communion of his flesh and his spirit.

'And so his whole life was spent in vain protests and futile attempts to readjust himself. His very logic makes him seem demented. The more he tries to achieve his own harmony, the greater his discord with society. The more he tries to make peace with himself, the more hostility he arouses around him ... And it is precisely his imperious *uprightness* of nature which makes him seem wayward and incoherent.... To judge him, we ought to be at the dead centre of his being.'

'Whence comes, then, the rebellion of a Nietzsche, a Dostoevsky, a Chestov?

'These are *religious* rebellions. The war which they wage against morality is essentially a religious war.' BORIS DE SCHLOEZER: Preface to Chestov's *Révélations de la mort*

'It is most often through traits which his own generation ignored or disliked that a writer contrives to speak to us across the ages. To pick out, among the preoccupations of one's own time, the things which will engage the interest of future generations: that is what calls for the rarest perspicacity.' ANDRÉ GIDE: Preface to an anthology of Montaigne

'I believe that lies may be momentarily useful, but that in the long run they necessarily do harm. Truth, on the other hand, must always be useful in the long run, although it may sometimes momentarily do harm. From this I should be tempted to conclude that the man of genius who calls attention to a widely-held misapprehension, or who first brings to our notice some great truth, is always deserving of veneration.

'It may sometimes happen that prejudice and the law mark him down as their victim.... But this ignominy cannot be lasting....' DIDÉROT: *Le Neveu de Rameau*

★

Gide always wants to *share* everything.

'Pleasure has no savour for me, where there is no communication: when I have even so much as a ribald passing thought, it annoys me if I have produced it by myself and have no one to whom to offer it.' MONTAIGNE, *(III, 9)*

ILE DE PORQUEROLLES, JULY 1922

Gide had announced his arrival for today.

Yesterday we were sitting beneath the pine trees in the late afternoon, at the hour when the *Cormoran*, which does the daily victualling run, comes back from the *presqu'île* of Gien. Without thinking, I trained my field-glasses upon her, and I was dumbfounded to see Gide, standing up, with his cape floating in the wind, quite by himself, in the prow of the little ship. Like a scene from Lohengrin.... In his affectionate haste, he had advanced his arrival by a whole day.

This morning at dawn he got up and went off at

random, tearing across the island like a drunken savage, half-naked, scratching himself on arbutus and tamarisk, chasing after butterflies, picking flowers, picking berries from the shrubs, plunging into every creek to find which was the warmest, jumping from rock to rock and fishing, in the narrow clefts, for seaweed, shells, and tiny sea-monsters that he brought back in his handkerchief. It was past twelve when he reappeared in the hotel dining-room, with sand in his ears and bits of sea-wrack all over his body, laughing, wild-eyed, drunk with light and heat and happiness and reciting, in his excitement, the lines of Heredia:

> *Le soleil, sous la mer, mys-té-ri-euse aurore,*
> *Eclaire la forêt des coraux abyssins ...!*

This afternoon he went to the draper's and bought himself an indescribable linen hat; he now can't be separated from it. And he's begun to work: the translation of Act I of *Hamlet*. But from time to time he can't help making for the sea; and off he goes through the pine trees, with that hat on the back of his head, and his arms full of books, notebooks, grammars and dictionaries. Then he comes back, deep in thought, and at once begins writing again.... As he splashed along the water's edge, he'd been looking for the equivalent of some English phrase ... and the amazing thing is: he's found it!

This afternoon I read to Gide a first version of *La gonfle*.

We were sitting at the water's edge, on the shady terrace of the empty villa. (Some days before Gide arrived, I had got permission to work there every day, in order to get away from our rooms at the hotel.)

Hardly had I begun to read when two very good-looking adolescent boys came across from the other side of the bay, some three hundred yards from us, and began to lounge about on the jetty; later, they went down to the rocks to bathe. Gide at once took up my binoculars. 'I'm still listening, Roger ... don't stop reading ... do go on....' I read for an hour, but he never once put down the binoculars. I read badly; I was angry and distressed; I felt that his attention was entirely taken up by the two naked boys who were playing about in the shallows, and whose cries and laughter were wafted up to us, from time to time, by the breeze. Gide would certainly have sold his soul to have the Devil drop my manuscript in the sea and leave him free to run to the jetty.... The moment I had finished the last act, he went off 'to stretch his legs', without saying a word about my play.

But this evening he discussed it with me at length, and with the greatest possible understanding. He had been listening to every word.

My first stay at Cuverville, the season notwithstanding. Gide brought me down from Paris.

Felt *most* uncomfortable throughout the journey....

It began the moment we got to Saint-Lazare. Gide —who is always having to make this journey—was wandering about the station, with no idea of where to buy his ticket, where to get on to the platform, what time the train left for Le Havre, or even if there was a connection that would allow us to catch the stopping train to Cricquetot. Unwilling to ask anybody anything, he ran from place to place with vague cries of: 'Let's try here ... come on ... just follow me....' We climbed at the very last moment on to a half-full train, which I hoped was the right one; and Gide at once began to behave as oddly as only he can. Swathed in an overcoat that he'd thrown across his shoulders, with a furry black hat perched on the very top of his head, his arms piled high with books and magazines, with a wild inquisitive gleam in his eye (and that winning, unde- cided smile, that spuriously natural air that he assumes in such cases, under the illusion that a free-and-easy manner will enable him to pass unnoticed) he made his way along the train, dragging me behind him along the ice-cold and largely deserted corridors. We did the whole distance several times—from the front coach to the guard's van, and *vice versa*. He scrutinised each carriage in turn, stopped wherever the compartment was at all full, tried one after another, turned against this one for some indecipherable reason, and that one from a motive that he did not disclose; and then, suddenly regretting one that he had decided against at the other end of the train, he hauled me off to look for it; but he couldn't find it, and so the whole thing began again. In the end I left him to his manoeuvres, and settled myself carefully in a corner seat of my own choosing. But I couldn't begin to read.

The discomfort I spoke of is very difficult to define; but it was made up of a double feeling, in which responsibility and insecurity both played a part. Some people would understand this; others wouldn't.... It's as if I had charge of a child who was on the point of committing the most ghastly imprudences ... or of an invalid with high fever....

There have been occasions during my visit to Cuverville when certain signs of distress, on the part of Madame Gide, have made me think back to this disagreeable journey. Signs? Hints, rather: sudden silences, moments of confusion that she tried quickly but unsuccessfully to conceal, and sometimes a flicker of anxiety, of fear almost, that vanished almost at once.... There are moments when, if her husband is in the room (and usually when he is at his best—gay, natural, and talkative), she seems to be walking on red-hot coals.

What happens within her, at such moments? What thoughts, what suspicions, what memories flash across her mind? I would swear that her momentary disquiet is like my own, and that my feeling of insecurity is something of which she has long experience—and that she sometimes feels it to the point of real anguish. How can one believe that this timid, delicate, all-fearing woman, with her conservative, her obstinately austere cast of mind, has ever found the least support in her capricious companion—that perpetual fugitive, with his disconcerting whims and his incapacity to re-sist temptation? What could be more injurious, more exhausting, for a balanced nature (even if, as is the case with Madame Gide, she is ready to welcome, within reason, the element of fantasy in human affairs) than to live side by side with this perpetual inconsequence, this perpetual submission to the unforeseeable? Even if there were no more serious ground for disagree-ment, that in itself would set up an intimate dishar-mony.

'I needn't say, my dear Roger, that you've made a con-quest of my wife,' Gide keeps on saying: he seems touched, as am I myself, by the extraordinarily gracious welcome which Madame Gide always extends to me.

I see her mostly at meals, and after dinner; she takes her part quite spontaneously in the conversation, and her contributions show great finesse of mind. Once again I note how oddly they behave to one another— that attentive politeness, that mixture of the easy and the studied that they introduce into every aspect of their relationship, the eager consideration which they show for one another, the tender affability, the smiling watchfulness ... and, at the same time, an impenetrable coldness beneath it all, a sharp fall in temperature in the depths: the absence, in fact, not merely of anything approaching the normal familiarity of marriage, but even of the intimacy which unites two friends, or two travelling companions. Their love for one another—patent as it is—remains distant, sublimated, uncommunicated; it is the love of two strangers who are never quite sure that they thoroughly know or thoroughly understand one another, and who never communicate with each other in the secret places of their hearts.

Once again, moreover, I was struck by the flashes of gaiety which sometimes dart, at the slightest pretext, across that face which is normally so serious, so tightly held-in. There is a touching contrast at such moments between the features, on which age has already left its mark, and the freshness, the pearly ring, the amazingly youthful—not to say childish—timbre of her laughter. Like a spring which bubbles up under dead leaves.... (There are old maids and grey-haired schoolmistresses who can never, one thinks, have been young; but they too have bursts of sudden, uncontrollable laughter in which one can glimpse the clear face of adolescence as it replaces, for a miraculous second, the mask of middle age.)

The house has great charm. It is plain and unluxurious in style, with the simplicity of a handsome middle-class house of the eighteenth century. Two storeys of small-paned windows in a long flat façade, unadorned save by the harmony of its lines, the distinction of its proportions, and the central pediment: a white triangle that stands out against a high slate roof. The plasterwork is pale yellow; and all the shutters, white.

To the left, a century-old plantation of beeches overlooks the garden, which is much longer than it is broad, and is divided in two: the front-door steps descend to a large lawn, shaded to the right by an enormous cedar (planted, Gide tells me, a hundred years ago by his grandfather, at the time when he bought the estate); on the other side is a romantic little park, with narrow paths that wind round grassy beds, each bearing the plants that Gide knows individually, and watches over, and tends with his own hands. Both façades look out on to open country; on one side and the other the view, to the far horizon, is that of the monotonous, wild, rather melancholy landscape of Normandy; a vast expanse of open fields, flat and bare, but varied occasionally by the beech avenues, those long and lofty oases that protect the farms from the rain-bearing winds blowing in from the Channel.

To the right of the imitation-marble hall, there is a drawing-room, with white wainscotting, and windows on both sides; it is not lived in in winter; but in high summer it must be charming, with its polished mahogany furniture, its *crédences*, its armchairs with flowered tapestry covers, its spick and span curtains, and its honey-coloured parquet; all this has been the same for the last hundred years. Farther on is the study; this also is not in use, and is full of apples and pears that have been laid out to ripen on wicker trays. To the left of the hall is the dining-room, the only room which is really lived in at the moment. There are three wicker chairs in front of the chimney-piece; a wood fire is kept burning the whole day—mainly, it would seem, on behalf of three huge Siamese cats. These majestic, ever sleepy animals, weighed down with their own fat and wrapped in their heavy coats of brown fur, may generally be found in occupation of the three chairs. The meals, devised with no great show of imagination, are copious in the extreme and served with an Anglo-Saxon regard for good form; we take them on a round table beside one of the windows. One of the doors leads off to the sanctuaries of the mistress of the house; the pantries, the dairy, the store-rooms for fruit and lamps and candles and oil, and the immense kitchen gleaming with coppery reflections like a Dutch picture. Madame Gide toils away there, hour after hour, among the heady smells of petrol and beeswax and turpentine. For the tyranny of spit and polish is absolute at Cuverville. Everything that can possibly be polished is mirror-bright. Flagstones, tiled floors, and parquets are perilous skating rinks. The staircase is the prime example: according to a rite which has been observed in its every detail for at least the last fifty years, housemaids, unhurried and armed with woollen dusters, inexhaustibly caress every surface, every relief, every nook and cranny—from the red tiles of the steps themselves, and their oaken surrounds, to the least projection of the wrought-iron banisters. An alluvial deposit, dating from several generations, a thick layer of hardened wax, transparent as varnish and gleaming like a topaz, gives the entire staircase the appearance of being sculpted from some polished, unidentifiable, and certainly costly material: from a block of brown amber.

(I call to mind the way in which Gide bivouacked in the villa at Auteuil, the dust, the unmade bed, the sink full of dirty china. . . . Here is just one of many details of life at Cuverville: Madame Gide has had dust-sheets specially made like loose covers, to fit over the bookshelves each morning while the rooms are being cleaned. . . .)

Gide lives above the kitchen, in two communicating rooms—the old woodwork a delicate greyish-green in colour. But he has a genius for discomfort: wherever he is, he seems to be merely passing through: his room at once takes on the air of a bivouac. Incongruous items of furniture are disposed haphazardly about the room, and put to some purpose remote from that for which they were designed. Access to the window is blocked by an old marble washstand, piled high with books; sheets and towels are crammed into a rose-wood secretaire; the straight-backed desk chair is used only as a rack for scarves and neckties. When working, he prefers to use a straw seated stool and a fragile occasional table, which he pushes almost into the ashes of the wretched fire, hardly warm enough to toast his shins, which burns in the grate. But, behind him, he has opened a large and elaborate tapestry screen. Madame Gide has sent up an armchair for me, and so it is more or less on top of the fire, and sheltered by the big screen, that we talk for days on end: marvellous days, days crowded with affection, and mutual trust, and general agreement—and, of course, with laughter and flights of fancy.

It is there that he read me the book he is working on this autumn—a first beginning of the *Faux-monnayeurs*. There are some excellent passages: some of the characters come off very well, there are fragments of stimulating dialogue, and the unsurpassable pages of Edouard's journal. But how much of it is empty and tedious! 'Lagoons' is our name for these dullnesses. Gide is disappointed with what he reads: he'd thought that, as a whole, the opening chapters were better than they are. But one can't be surprised: he refuses to work according to a prearranged plan. He himself doesn't know where he's going, nor even—with any certainty—where he wants to go. He writes on impulse, according to the whim of the moment. In the middle of a chapter, and to strengthen some incident—or sometimes just to find room for a telling scrap of dialogue—he will invent a new character whom he'd never thought of before; he's tempted by an outline that happens to suggest itself—but as to whom it belongs to, or what part it will play in the story, or whether he can find some rôle for it to assume, he hasn't the least idea. Of course I won't stand for this.

Construction above all things! I quote what Bourdelle says: 'Harmonious construction is the secret of everything: faulty proportions can never be redeemed by details.' Gide protests, and casts about for ways of defending his haphazard methods of composition. The fact is that he likes it because it amuses him. But my case is the stronger: the results leave too much to be desired. He hadn't realised that, but he has to admit that it's true. Not without argument, though. We argue gaily, warmly, till we're quite out of breath.... I express myself badly, I hesitate, I seem to contradict myself the whole time; but fundamentally I have a pretty strong grasp of what I want to say, and Gide is so clever with his dialectical forceps that he always gets it out of me in the end. I don't always convince him; but my sincerity is always useful, and when he isn't persuaded, he at least emerges with a more conscious understanding of his own point of view.

(I believe that that is one of the secrets, one of the most stable bases of our understanding and our intimacy. Two men of good faith confront one another; the one driven blindly forward by the need to bring out, at whatever cost, the quintessence of his thoughts; the other, prompted by an incredible modesty—and one which neither age nor fame has been able to modify—who takes a pleasure—a slightly masochistic pleasure, perhaps—in allowing himself to be criticised as soon as he recognises an honesty which he knows to be authentic and disinterested.)★

An example of Gide's extraordinary emotional sensitivity:

One evening, when the three of us were sitting by the fire, he suggested that he should read to Madame Gide and myself a 'remarkable' article by his uncle, Charles Gide. (It was about the unveiling of the war memorials, and had appeared in last December's *Emancipations*. 'Uncle Charles' declared among other things that all those pre-1914 politicians, who had been powerless to prevent the disaster, and who now have the effrontery to raise their voices before the graves of our soldiers, should confine themselves to the two words: 'Forgive us!')

When he read this passage, Gide was so moved that he had to interrupt himself time and time again. He

★Gide's *Journal*: *November 19th 1924*. Read to R.M.G. the last chapters I had written. To see my book reflected in a mind so different from my own brings out the defects of the book, and also its qualities.... How much work remains to be done, if I am to bring to a successful conclusion what has already been so much worked upon!

December 24th 1931. With R.M.G. I can let myself go and be perfectly natural. There is nobody whose presence now brings me greater comfort.... With him, I never feel that I am wasting my time....

was literally suffocated by his fits of weeping. His voice quavered to such an extent that we could hardly make out what he was saying; and his tie was soaked with the huge childlike tears which rolled down his badly shaven cheeks and met under his chin.

Madame Gide's attitude seemed to me significant. She was moved, admittedly, but she was still more surprised, and it was clear that she was embarrassed. Because of me, perhaps? At once touched by an excess of sensibility, whose sincerity was beyond question, and deeply shocked by the immodesty of so great a failure of restraint, of 'self-control', as the English say.*

At nightfall on the day before I left I made a moving pilgrimage with Gide. The air was icy cold, and heavy with rain; the garden dripped water everywhere, and was already half-hidden in shadow. 'Here is the *bench*,' said Gide, and he gripped my arm. 'The bench in the *Porte étroite*. . . . And here is the *little gate* that leads to the kitchen garden. . . . That wrings my heart, so intensely did I live those minutes with

*Graphology. . . . I note, though I draw no conclusion from it, what I remember particularly of Madame Gide's handwriting: that it was firm, upright, and well-drawn at the beginning of each word; but untidy, shaky, and formless, at the end. It is as if the energy required for the first letters collapsed after each brief effort, and was then revived by an ephemeral act of the will at the beginning of the next word.

Alissa.... She opens the door, and Jerome is waiting there—there, in the shadows. "Is that you, Jerome?" she asks.... Ah, Roger, how lovely all that is! And yet it stifles me. I walk here like a ghost, in a past that is gone for ever. My life is lived in other places now.'

He takes me off towards the village, along a grass-grown, sopping wet, slithery path. We bog down in it, but Gide doesn't mind. 'It's a little marshy here, but never mind ... I'd like to show you ... this part of the country is quite unlike any other, isn't it?' And suddenly he leaves me, springs up the bank, and vanishes for a moment under the trees. A little way off I can see, through the foliage, a window with a light in it. Gide is back with me already: 'I went to see if the stream had overflowed.... Come with me, and I'll show you our village....' But before we get to the first houses, he breaks off at a right angle and plunges across the fields. 'Let's go back this way....' He goes on in front, with big strides; I have quite a job to keep up with him. When we get to a sunken lane, with hedges on either side, he goes faster still. I'm ankle-deep in the ruts, soaked with rain, running with sweat. In the darkness ahead of me I hear Gide's affectionate voice: 'Lovely, isn't it? It's well worth a little wetting.' Night has come on and we can see nothing of the country. Gide is ploughing on, and almost at a run, when he stops short. Through a gap in the embankment I can see a light among the trees. 'Let's push on to there, shall we?' He turns to the right, and plunges headlong up a muddy farm track. Is it the cottage that he wanted to see, a little while ago, from the top of the slope? Is it to come back there that we've made this appalling detour?

It's a sort of barn, with a decrepit thatched roof that stands out against the pallor of the sky. He opens the door. What we see inside would make most people shut it again. A spindly child of ten or eleven is seated, reading, by the light of a flickering lamp, at a table covered with potato peel. Opposite him stands a stocky, big-bellied girl, ragged, filthy, with protruding eyes and scanty hair. She is peeling potatoes in a dazed sort of way, and is at least six months gone with child. How old is she? Fifteen? Twenty? Twenty-five? On the mud floor are two palliasses, two heaps of rag, on which three flea-ridden children—the youngest not more than a year old—are climbing about. Gide goes straight over to the table and strokes the boy's head, as if he were a little dog. 'Hullo, Barnabé! Working, are you? Let's see ... wait while I get my glasses.... Ah, the decimal system! Difficult, isn't it? ... That's good, though ... that's very good.... We were just passing, my friend and I ... we came to pay you a little visit.... Your father not back yet? Well, well ... and how are the babies? Still got impetigo, have they? ...' The boy hasn't looked up; he is watching me from under his lashes, without saying a word. It is his sister who, with an inane smile, brings out a 'Yes, *m'sieu.* . . .'

We go out into the wet wind and the night. Gide walks beside me, in silence, at a leisurely pace.

'You see,' he says at last. 'Very interesting, isn't it? The most squalid poverty. . . . He is charming, that little Barnabé, don't you think? But they're all eaten up with lice. . . . The mother died of tuberculosis a long time ago . . . the father works on a farm. He makes a good living, but he drinks. They never have a penny in the house. My wife gives them something, three times a week. . . . They say that the father sleeps with the daughter—the half-witted one, did you notice her? She stammers. . . . I don't know if my wife realises. . . . He's charming, that boy, with his poor lined sickly face. . . . Well, that's how things are, round here. I know a lot of families like that. . . . My wife takes them some sheets, or a shirt or two, and the next day they're filthy or torn to bits . . . there's nothing to be done . . . it's incurable. . . . All the same he's very endearing, that little Barnabé!'

Then he falls silent again, till we reach the house.

But when we reach the garden gate he turns to me with a laugh:

'Guess what they call me, in the village? I found it out—oh, ten years ago, at least. . . . I was bicycling back from Criquetot. At the beginning of the holidays. I passed by the school just when the children were coming out. And I saw all the little girls laughing, and pointing to me, and calling out to one another: "Oh, look! Look! Here's the Idiot come back again!"' He is chortling with laughter. 'Yes, Roger, the whole village has nicknamed me the Idiot! Isn't it enchanting? Straight out of Dostoevsky, isn't it?'★

JANUARY 1924

Gide: 'There's not a day, there's hardly an hour nowadays, when I don't think of my death. Not in a romantic way, mark you. Not at all: I feel that I'm faced with something *evident*. . . . Wherever I go—if I pay a call, or take a bath, or go into a cake shop, or ride in a bus—the idea suddenly occurs to me: "What if I were to die here and now?" Sometimes I think: "Here would do very well." But usually it's: "Oh Heavens—

★Gide's way of laughing is quite peculiar to himself. Plain uncontrollable laughter is unknown to him. But when he tells a story that delights him, either by its pungency or by its fun, his voice climbs up to an unbelievable falsetto, becomes very thin in timbre, and then suddenly strangles itself in a sodden 'glou-glou'; the cheeks fill out with a quite abnormal quantity of saliva; the lower lip falls, points forward, and opens like the basin of a little fountain; meanwhile, through the narrow slit of the screwed-up eyelids, the laughing and almost invisible gaze is fixed on his interlocutor with an expression of the intensest curiosity and jubilation.

not on any account!" And I hurry off somewhere else.... I'm not distressed by this obsession, but it quickens my taste for life, makes me even readier than usual to avoid people who would otherwise take up my time, and things that would restrict or encumber me ... to say "No", in fact, to everything that takes time from *my own ends*.'

'I love the whole of life, and detest one thing only: that my nature should be irreparably confined to one arbitrary form, even if that form is of my own choosing.'
AMIEL

MARCH 1924

Stayed with Gide in the Var, at La Bastide. An atmosphere of affectionate well-being. Gide has never seemed gayer or more unaffectedly happy.

The house is full: for lack of space, he and I share a room. Morning and evening, interminable conversations as we lie in our respective beds. He laughs at my manias; I, at his. For instance I've discovered that he sleeps wrapped in a sort of white dressing-gown, thick and cottony, of which the skirts come down to his ankles, like a baker's apron; and round his waist he winds, as tightly as he can (so that it squeezes his diaphragm), a big black silk scarf, nine feet in length! He looks like a Grand Panjandrum in half mourning. . . .

It's amusing to come upon Gide when he's playing with his daughter . . . or rather when he bends, with the patient curiosity of the entomologist, above this baby of ten months as it wriggles and crawls along the carpet. What interests him is the spontaneity of the child, its reflexes, the smallest indications of the first instincts of this precocious little being, with her shining watchful eyes, her strange way of lowering her head to hide her smile. Already she has such a passionate desire for whatever objects are beyond her grasp that she clenches her fists, and her hands tremble, and move to and fro, and stretch out in an ecstasy of longing; until her whole body writhes and shudders in a sort of interior delirium. Gide is beside himself with delight: he never wearies of watching her excitement. Above all he insists that the baby should not be moved nearer to the object she desires. Whatever she does, nobody must interfere. He is almost annoyed: 'Oh, do leave her alone! . . . It's so interesting! . . . Let her do as she likes. . . . *Just to see. . . .*'

1924

Gide's every moment must be put to use.

There is nothing of the idler about Gide, with his

poetry, his sensuality, his independence of thought and action. There's not a minute of the day, not a moment of his sleepless nights, when his mind is on holiday and his brain stops producing the raw material of his books.... Gide is a *man of letters*, from morning till night. Even in love, even in making love.... The most fleeting impressions are captured at once, translated into Gidian terms, and condensed into a formula stamped with his personal seal, so that they can be used at any time. The only aim of his life is to enrich his work (or to enrich himself—but himself *on behalf of* his work). Gide seems to intoxicate himself at random—to gorge himself on every flower. But look more closely: from every raid he returns with fresh honey for the hive.

DECEMBER 1924

Visited Gide in the sanatorium at Reuilly. He has acute appendicitis, and must be operated on at once.

He's never been operated on before. Rightly or wrongly, and though he has little pain, he is convinced he won't get over it. I found him flat on his back, motionless, with a bag of ice on his stomach. His face was pale, curiously youthful, and much better-looking; his eyes were clear and candid; on his lips was the smile of a well-behaved schoolboy. He spoke of nothing but his will and his last wishes. When he thinks things out, he knows quite well that he's not condemned to death; but his whole being, body and mind alike, is making ready, in spite of himself, to die. He himself is amazed that he should accept the idea of dying with so little protest.

'The thing is,' he said to me, 'that I really died, within myself, several years ago, when I found that my wife had burnt all my letters, the better to detach herself from me, the better to cut me quite out of her life.... When someone has suffered what I suffered then, my dear Roger, the rest is nothing....'

And, after a silence:

'I think of her all the time. She will never know it....'

1925

I re-read the *Cahiers d'André Walter*.

In 1877, at the age of eighteen, Gide was already writing: 'For my part, there is not one of my desires that does not shake my being to its very foundations....'

And this, addressed to Emmanuèle. She could have read it––and she undoubtedly did read it—a few years before their marriage: 'I do not desire you. Your body is an embarrassment to me, and I have been always horrified by physical possession.'

★

'I do not give the name of kindness,' Benjamin Constant wrote at the end of *Adolphe*, 'to that ephemeral pity which cannot dominate impatience, or prevent it from re-opening the wounds which a moment of regret has stanched. *The great question in life is the pain that one causes*, and not even the most ingenious metaphysics can justify the man who has broken the heart that loved him.'

JUNE 1926

Just back from Paris, where I went for a few days to see Gide on his return from the Congo.

I arrived at the Villa Montmorency on Monday morning. The door was ajar. The big hall was empty and dusty, and cluttered up, like a left luggage office, with all the impedimenta of the expedition: twenty rusted tin trunks, and a score of chests, boxes, and strange battered bundles, stained with mud, and exuding a strong and sickly smell. . . .

'Hallo there!' I cried into the wings. A distant voice replied 'Hallo!' and Gide came running and took me in his arms. He had on a jacket of a very light beige in colour—a loose woollen affair—and round his neck a red foulard which made him look very pale. He seemed changed—his features weary and strained, his glance evasive; but it wasn't easy to examine him, because he kept hiding his face from me. Can it be emotion which makes him timid? He took me into the dining-room, where the remains of breakfast were still on the table. He started to put everything away. And just as I was saying 'But do let me look at you a moment ...' he replied, as he handed me one end of the tablecloth, 'Help me to fold this, will you, Roger?'

A wood fire, despite the season, kept the temperature up to hot-house level in the room in which he has lived since he came back. He sits there in the cosy seclusion of the huge chimney-piece, on a low chair; beside him is a little table covered with letters and newspaper articles. Not a single book. On the floor, within reach, is a great heap of logs that he has brought up himself from the cellar and piled on a foundation of newspapers.

Giving me a chair, he at once—as if we had only parted the day before—began to speak: not of his journey, not of the Congo or the Chad or the equatorial forest, not of his stay with Marcel de Coppet, but entirely about Parisian literary life, the gossip of the N.R.F., certain accusations that have been made against him, the reviews of his *Faux-monnayeurs* and all the inaccuracies, the misleading interpretations, and the disobliging allusions which he has detected and is impatient to contravert. I thought that he would come back from Africa like a traveller returned from the planet Sirius, and that it would take months for him to re-adapt himself to the petty dramas of our everyday life.... I was rather disappointed to see him so quick, and so eager, to plunge into the inferno of literary 'shop' and the wrangles of the monthly reviews.... He was on edge, restless, for ever getting up and sitting down again, lighting cigarettes and putting them out, tying and untying his foulard, or bending down to poke the fire. I could sense that this unhealthy, feverish condition kept him constantly on the very edge of exasperation. I therefore suggested that I should cut short my visit. He held me back. And—still without asking any questions of me, or allowing me to put any to him—he at last began to speak of the great problem which preoccupies him: his report on the injustices and abuses which he discovered in Africa. Once launched, he began to expound the whole problem of colonisation, put the questions in their right order, marshalled the arguments, became more and more excited, and raised his voice. I noted that he spoke in quite an unwonted way—solemnly, eloquently, persuasively; his phrasing took on an oratorical turn: 'Far be it from me to claim ... I think that we now have ample proof ... But you may perhaps wish to put the opposite view....' He must have noticed this, for he interrupted with a smile and said: 'I'm not boring you, my dear Roger? Because all this is really most useful to me, you know. . . . It's a sort of first draft that I'm making in front of you. . . .'

(I also note this incident, which shows to what a degree his sensibilities were exacerbated by the exhausting return journey. At one moment he opened a dossier and began to read me an official report, *dated 1902*. This describes the miserable plight of a native tribe—I forget which one—which had been decimated by famine and ruined by taxation and the changing conditions of transport. He reached a passage which I transcribe from memory: 'Abandoning their villages and their derelict farms, the people fled in great numbers to the bush, where they kept themselves alive by eating roots. . . .' And there he stopped dead, literally strangled by the strength of his feelings. Twice he swallowed, wiped his eyes, and tried hard to take hold of himself and continue his reading; but then, unable to contain his tears, he handed me the report, and stammered out: 'Read it . . . I can't go on. . . .' He then got up and staggered off into another room. Left alone, I read the phrase which had so greatly distressed him. Here it is, word for word: '. . . until the majority succumbed in an epidemic of recurrent fever'.

But all this happened in 1902—twenty-four years ago. . . .)

★

Might not one say of the *Nourritures* what Saint-Beuve says somewhere of certain books: that they are "useful", but that their life is short, because "the generations which profit by them are also the generations which exhaust them"?

★

'Never confuse the real man, the man who wrote the book, with the man whom the book calls to mind.'
VALÉRY: *Variété*.

1928

Gide is being spoilt by the complaisance of his entourage. He no longer pays the least attention to the preoccupations, the desires, the troubles, or the tastes of anyone but himself. He can hardly conceive that somebody should not, at any given moment, be free. And by 'free' he means: ready to give up everything in order to put oneself entirely at his disposition; ready, not only to visit him, but to share, for the inside of a day, his life, his work, his pleasures, and his meals; ready to enter into the most trifling of his anxieties; ready to speak of the subjects which preoccupy him, to the exclusion of all others; ready to laugh, if he is in the mood to be amused; or to wax indignant, if he has some pretext for annoyance or chagrin; ready to sit patiently with a newspaper or a magazine while he has his siesta; ready to read the letters he has just received, and to discuss with him the answers that he has prepared; ready to read on with him in the book he has already begun; ready to go out, if he takes it into his head to go to an exhibition, or a cinema, or to call on a colleague. . . . He is never more affectionate than when he wishes, at all costs, to keep you with him: 'No, don't go, my dear Roger! We've still got so much to say to one another! Light your pipe and come along with me. I simply must have a shave.' He'd drag me right into the bathroom and make me watch him while he shaved, if I didn't slip away when his back was turned.

(How unjust I am! And how shameful of me to give way to that moment of bad temper! Have I ever spent an hour with him, and not been the richer for it? Even on his most tyrannical days he finds an opportunity, twenty times over, of giving more than he gets. He gives fresh life to everything he touches. He talks as the sower sows; and the seeds that he scatters all round him ask only to be allowed to take root, and to flower.)

1928

I cannot approve of the susceptibility which now makes him resentful, not merely of attacks, but of the smallest inaccuracy on the part of any critic, and of any interpretation, however trivial, that he considers erroneous or disobliging. . . .

After having been unknown and misunderstood for more than thirty years—and after having endured those years with the noblest, proudest, most uncomplaining resignation—he now cannot resist the temptation of taking his revenge. And so it is that the all-echoing little world of letters is ringing with the noise of his complaints and his controversies. How I should like to see him meet such things with greater detachment—with indifference, in fact!★

(Also he is preoccupied with the image of himself that he wishes to leave behind him. He wants to compose it himself, and to force it upon the public. I'm very much afraid that it's a waste of his time; we shall none of us supervise the modelling of our own death-mask....)

1931

In the *Nouvelles Littéraires* for March 7th, André Suarès says of Goethe:

'He has no use for anyone—even if he acknowledges his merits—who can contribute nothing towards the evolution of Goethe.'†

★A lady whom we both know once said to me: 'We oughtn't to want him to correct even the least of his oddities; he'd lose all his virtues at the same time.'

†'Or to his pleasure' I should add if I wanted to apply this to Gide.

'The word "pathological" can only be applied to what is unproductive,' Stefan Zweig wrote. In his preface to *Amok*, Romain Rolland makes the following comment:

'Wherever the abnormal is a principle of strength, and a source of creation, it is not abnormal at all, but super-normal.'

JULY 30TH 1931

I found Gide in a terrible state. He showed me a pamphlet in which he is accused of perverting young people. There is nothing that moves him to greater transports of distress, indignation, and despair.

'Perverting young people! As if we don't know very well, by the way, what these so-called normal people understand by that phrase! And what they always imagine.... When they run after a woman, it's possession they're after. And so they assume that anyone who seeks to win the love of a young boy is simply out to corrupt him. That's as far as their imagination goes! "Perverting young people" really means "making young perverts of them"—profiting by their easygoing, all-accepting natures.... How can I defend myself? How can I persuade them that as far as I'm concerned—and I'm not an exception—nothing could be farther from the truth? They'd laugh in my face if I assured them that never, never.... If I could only speak out! If I could give names and dates—real case-histories—they'd see to what an extent their accusations are unjust! How often have I been held back by the respect that I feel for a young life! Often I've waited for months before accepting love, when it was offered to me.... Perverting young people! As if it were perverse to initiate a human being in the pleasures of making love! As a rule, it's quite the opposite! People forget—or rather, they never know—the background of those caresses. Friendships of that kind are born and come to fruition in an atmosphere of confidence, and loyalty, and noble emulation.... Believe me, my dear Roger—I can say this for myself: that my influence on the young people who have come to me has always been healthy and beneficial. And that's not a paradox: my stand has always been on the side of morality. I've always striven to awaken, or to develop, their consciences; I've always managed to heighten and strengthen whatever was best in their natures. How often had those boys already become the victims of bad habits—and it was I who brought them back to the narrow path: but for me, they'd have abandoned themselves to their basest instincts and been lost for ever! How many recreants, idlers, hypocrites and liars have been inspired by my counsels to form a taste for hard work, and order, and beauty, and straightforwardness! And all thanks to

nothing but this reciprocated attraction and this reciprocated tenderness. . . . But how could I make them understand?'

He mentioned names, described individual cases,
put forward one example after another. He grew grad-
ually more and more fevered as he once again expounded his ideas and sang the praise of the 'love of
the Greeks', as he calls it. He claims that in the trou-
bled years of adolescence nothing can replace the good
influence of an attachment—a physical, moral and intellectual attachment—with an older man who is deserving of love and confidence. It is the revelations of
an older companion which can best help a boy to cross,
unharmed and in an atmosphere of masculine, broth-
erly enthusiasm, the redoubtable threshold of puberty.
Only an initiation of this kind can turn him away from
the pernicious temptations of the street and spare him
the sordid and dangerous discoveries which lie in wait
'on the prostitute's bed'. . . . (Gide has still, among the
relics of his puritan education, a wild terror of those
illnesses which we associate with the name of Venus!)

JULY 1ST 1932

Rejoined Gide at Cassis-sur-Mer, where he was waiting for me.

The idea of his death never leaves him; it is the basis of his thoughts, and the *leit-motif* of his conversa-

tion. 'Not that I want to die, my dear Roger ... But there are moments, very often, when I no longer wish to live.'

I press him to explain himself further. He speaks of the rapid evolution of the world, of ideas, and of institutions. He admits to finding all this hard to follow, and to feeling out of date amongst it all. He realises full well that he will not live to see the completion of those social changes for which he longs with all his strength; and it is partly the knowledge of this which detaches him from life. He goes on, after a pause: 'That is why I am involving myself so deeply, so *imprudently*' (his own word) 'in the Communist Party.'★

JULY 2ND

This morning, he talked to me about his funeral. Haunted by the wish to spare his wife any painful ordeals, he would like her to have to take no initiative in the matter, to have no decision to make as to either the place or the form of his obsequies, and to be sheltered from the gaze of those others who may attend the ceremony. In any case he is anxious that only a very few

★He means, I think, that if he were twenty years old, and had a whole lifetime to 'stake' in the communist adventure, no doubt he would hesitate more, and no doubt his zeal would be tempered with a little more circumspection. But, at his age, a certain blindness in his adhesion seems to him less important.

friends should be present, and that no speeches should be made.

He asked me a great many questions about the procedure and the formalities of cremation.

I said to him:

'What does it matter to you? Why should you bother to decide in advance what is to be done when you are dead?'

He replied:

'Because I want to be, in death, as I have been in life. I want no religious demonstration of any kind, I want a secular burial, and a private one.'*

*André Gide had very often spoken of these matters in the firmest way in front of other friends, and in front of myself. It was with these declarations in mind that I could not help protesting vehemently (as did Jean Schlumberger and others), on the day of his funeral, against the undesirable presence of a pastor. This pastor had been brought from Le Havre at the request of Gide's family to welcome the body at the Château de Cuverville, to read aloud some verses from the Bible, to evoke the mystical (and ephemeral) flights of 'Numquid et tu . . .', to take his place at the head of the procession, to accompany the coffin to the cemetery in orthodox religious style, and finally to pray aloud at the side of the grave.

These protests might, in view of the place and the circumstances, have been called inopportune . . . but it is beyond all possible doubt that Gide would have approved of them.

'The excess of any particular virtue is admirable, in mankind, only where it is accompanied by the excess of the virtue which is directly opposed to it.' PASCAL

'His is a synthetic, a symphonic genius,' writes Léon Blum of Jean Jaurès. 'A genius remarkable above all for the diversities and the contradictions which mingle within it; for its power to make a harmonious living whole of thoughts and notions which, until Jaurès existed, had seemed discordant or even directly opposed. And Jaurès had to do it, because there existed within him, in perfect harmony, elements which are more or less never found in the same man.'

1933

'When we pass judgment on him,' writes Denise Fontaine of a character in the *Rivages de néant*, 'we do it according to a scale which was never intended for him. We are quite ready to admit that he's a great man, but we want him to be great *in our way*! We expect him to go further than ourselves, but we want him to go further along the same road! We admire him for being different, and yet we are appalled to find that he's not like ourselves!

'. . . He brings to life a form of perfection which I have never encountered in anyone else.'

An amusing conversation about the antithesis between the Dorian and the Ionic in art. According to Gide, these symbolise the two eternal currents of art. . . . Among the Dorians he lumps together Rabelais, Corneille, Molière, Rude . . . and himself (*sic*). Among the Ionians: Clodion, Carpeaux, Renan, etc. . . . 'It's true,' he added, 'that they've also got Racine on their side. . . .'—'And Barrès?' 'Barrès? Oh come now, Roger—he's a pure Ionian! He owes much more to Renan than to Chateaubriand. . . .' 'And Montaigne?' 'Ah, Montaigne! He's a great embarrassment to me. I really believe that the wretch managed to straddle both currents. . . .'

NICE: APRIL 1934

Gide has just left, after coming to spend several days here, in order to read to me a long fragment from his *Geneviève*, which was written in Syracuse last February.

He had a cold of sorts and was rather out of humour. . . . What he read to me could not possibly be called good. It was an interminable passage in which he dwells ponderously upon the *Foyer Franco-Belge*. (This was an institution to which, during the war, with the help of Madame van Rysselberghe and Charlie du Bos, Gide devoted three whole years; his perseverance and devotion to the *Foyer* deserved high praise.) It was an excellent opportunity to make a full-length portrait of Charlie; but this portrait is far too heavily accented. It is at once literal and something of a caricature—ferocious in parts, grating in others, quite amusing here and there, but really quite out of place in the book. When he read it aloud, Gide himself could see how heavy and inopportune it was. Egged on by me, he admitted that he'd taken to this novel 'for lack of anything better'—because, in fact, he had no work on hand, at that moment, which really tempted him. But he doesn't really know what he wants to put into it. There are a great many sketches, but none of them is any good; he can't manage to define the subject exactly, or to invent an appropriate story, or even to get the characters quite straight; the whole thing is shapeless, formless. . . .

These rather discouraging conclusions cast a shadow over our conversations. Our friendship is warmer, more expansive, more efficacious, and altogether works better, when we have good reason to be satisfied with one another, and are not too dissatisfied with ourselves. He left in a pretty disconsolate frame of mind—resolved, as it seemed, to abandon this projected *Geneviève*, which he has dragged about with him for years, and which is like one of those fruits, too early picked, which moulder and mummify instead of ripening.

As against all that, we had a great many interesting conversations about public events—politics, Communism, and so on. I took care not to say so, but I believe he is already beginning to react against his recent position. He's putting on the brakes. With the 'comrades' he often lets himself go far beyond the limits he'd set for himself. With me, he keeps hold of the reins and is more suspicious of his moments of enthusiasm; he looks into himself quite candidly. One thing he makes no attempt to hide, either from me or from himself: he is less of a convinced Communist than people think and say; the difference is certainly greater than his new militant friends would like him to suppose. I don't mean to insinuate that he is falling out of sympathy with the Russian experiment, or that he is losing confidence in the future of Marxism. But his critical sense remains very sharp; he has the liveliest natural repugnance to all dogmatic systems; and he has too inveterate a taste for his own form of unstable equilibrium—for the balanced entertainment of several contradictory points of view. All this makes it impossible for him to be at his ease among the intransigent unquestioning certainties of Communism. The Party must have been either very sure of itself, or very badly informed, when it put its money on Gide.... How imprudent they were to set such a value on the affiliation of one who is by nature so perfectly unconvinced, and who never holds the same view from one day to the next! I am very much afraid that in the long run, and for all his genuine goodwill, he will one day disappoint his new friends.

Renan reproached Victor Hugo for his lack of interest in History. 'That can only lead,' he said, 'to an immense lacuna in one's opinions.'

1934

I alluded to a malicious article in which X. had meant to give a word-portrait of Gide.

'Yes,' he said, with a laugh. 'Everyone who doesn't know me recognised me at once.'

1934

Gide is not invariably unbiassed in his judgments.

In serious matters, he generally displays a scrupulous conscience and a courageous integrity. But in little things he is not always so nice.... He is capable, for instance, of passing a final judgment upon a book that he has opened by chance and merely skimmed. He is capable of condemning, unread, a magazine whose policy he knows to be opposed to his own, of being unjust towards a review which is directed by Roman Catholics, and of being indulgent, *a priori*, towards one which is Protestant in its inspiration. He is capable, where a critic has wounded him, ten years ago, by some iniquitous judgment, of suspecting all that critic's later work—and without troubling to verify his suspicion. . . . (He is also capable of forgetting an insult to such a point that he will go and offer his hand, in all eager affection, to the cad who six months earlier had rolled him in the mud— -and when someone points out his mistake he will burst out laughing. . . .)

1937

'I am always on my guard when I experience a wave of lyricism . . . much too much so! . . . You know,' said Gide, after a pause, 'I believe that, if there is one quality which is mine and nobody else's, it is precisely this: that I can abandon myself to the wildest lyricism without losing my foothold or modifying in any way my vision of reality. . . . Yes, I can say today, in all sincerity, that my faculty of exaltation has never prevented me from seeing things as they are. I have the gift—and as I grow older I am convinced that it is quite uncommon—of combining at the same moment two states of mind as different, and as contradictory, as passion and lucidity; or as the fever, the delirium, the inward tremor of lyricism, and the chill of Reason . . .'

'To love intelligent women is a pederast's pleasure.'
BAUDELAIRE: *Journaux Intimes.*

1937

Some of us are wondering if, since the *Faux-monnayeurs*, Gide has not gone astray. . . . The *Ecole des femmes* and, more recently, the *Nouvelles nourritures*, leave us unsatisfied.

His adventure into politics gives proof of his courage, and of his natural generosity: but, also, of his frivolity. He had discovered the 'social question' during his journey to the Congo, and had remained deeply preoccupied with it. He tried to read *Das Kapital*. (For months on end he went about with a volume of Marx in his pocket: it was as if he'd set himself an imposition.) It was not political conviction that led him to Communism, but the hope and fervour *of the evangelist*. And it is as a disappointed evangelist that he turned away from it. The same candour marks adhesion and withdrawal alike. . . .

'Action does not interest me so much for the sensations it gives as for its consequences, its reverberations. That is why—though it interests me intensely—I think that it interests me all the more when it is committed by somebody else. I'm afraid, d'you see, of compromising myself: that is, of restricting what I might do in the future by what I am doing now. To think that, because I have done *this*, I could no longer do *that*—such thoughts are becoming intolerable to me. I would rather make others act than act myself.' GIDE: *Conversation avec un Allemand. N.R.F.*, August 1919

1937

Gide's indiscretion.

It saddens me to note that Gide's relations with his best friends are becoming more and more one-sided. We cannot feel for him the trusting confidence which he feels for us. Our reserves derive in part, of course, from our embarrassment at finding, in his *Journal*, such frequent allusions to our conversations with Gide; but worse than this is the exasperation (or the serious inconvenience) which he provokes by his continual indiscretion in everyday life!

Those quirks of his, those private obsessions are becoming altogether too much of a tyranny....

He is for ever brooding over himself, entirely preoccupied with his little misfortunes. I don't say that
they're not real, and I don't say that he cultivates them;
but he exaggerates their importance; he suffers from
them more than is necessary, and he makes those
around him suffer too. It's quite true that he has in-
somnia, and that he needs, after luncheon, to have
what he calls his 'napping'; but does this siesta really
require him to try, one after another, *all* the beds and
all the sofas? And need he exact a silence so complete
that the life of the whole house is paralysed for more
than an hour? It's true that he has to watch his liver;
but he uses this, when at table, as a pretext for stopping
all other conversation, while he digresses solemnly,
subtly, but quite uninterestingly about the quality of
each dish: the food has to be at once easy to digest and
exquisite in taste—for Gide, when he eats, is as fastid-
ious as a cat.... It's true that he's subject to colds and
to laryngitis, and that he has to take care to avoid sudden changes of temperature. But these precautions
have become a veritable obsession. Gide puts on too
many clothes, for fear that it may turn cold, and then
takes them off at the wrong moment for fear of break-
ing out in a sweat; consequently he never stops putting

on, taking off, and putting on again his innumerable waistcoats, pullovers, scarves, gaiters, and mittens; and his legs are constantly wriggling in and out of the rugs and supernumerary overcoats that he drags everywhere with him.... At the cinema it's nothing unusual for him to change his seat three or four times during the film, either to get nearer to the radiators, or to edge away from them, or perhaps to avoid some emergency exit which, if by any chance it were to open, would expose him to an insidious draught. I remember how once, when we went to see a film at the Récamier Cinema, he borrowed a handkerchief from me; when the lights went up I was amazed to find that my handkerchief had been knotted at its four corners and transformed into a bonnet, to the great amusement of our neighbours. Another time, at Nice, he whispered to me in the dark that he had been over-cautious enough to put on two pairs of under-pants: 'If you would be good enough to help me just a very little, my dear Roger ... we might just manage, while it's dark, and if we're very discreet. ...' I had to threaten to leave him flat if he persevered a second longer in his weird plan to take off his trousers on the sly. ...

Unfortunately I am weak enough to care about 'what other people think' ... To go out with Gide, today, is to risk making oneself the object of general curiosity; and that is torture to me.... When we are

alone, and in his house, I do more than support his ec-
centricities; they amuse me, I tease him about them,
we make jokes of them, and he laughs as much as I do.
They have come to form a traditional diversion or hilarious interval in our talks. (I suddenly see him fum-
bling with his cuffs; he coughs, and clears his throat;
he stops listening; he looks about him with an air of
anxious enquiry: 'Lost your mittens? There they are—
they've fallen into the folds of your shawl. . . .' I hand
them to him; he at once calms down, and we resume
our conversation with renewed excitement.)

1937
'There are some rather fine things in it. . . . What a pity
that he wasn't the first to say them.' DIDEROT: *Le Neveu de Rameau*

Beware of the 'stylist'! There's no one to equal him for
faked originality of thought—for the representation,
in new and unrecognisable dress, of ideas that are fa-
miliar to us from other sources.

In Gide's case there is a double disguise, and as the
one operates at a different time from the other, it is es-
pecially difficult to unmask him.

To begin with, the natural gait of his mind is quite
unlike anybody else's; he never thinks quite straight;
he always attacks his ideas from the side. (From his own

side, I admit—which is already an originality; but we must not confuse originality of procedure with originality of aim; there's nothing exploratory about taking an unfrequented side-road in order to get to a point which is already known.) This natural cast of his mind has enabled him, as we all know, to make certain invaluable discoveries; but they don't always come off. And when, as a result of some involuntary reminiscence, he goes to work upon something that has already been said, he merely gives a deceptive appearance of novelty to the hackneyed idea that Gide has taken over as his own. (In the same way, the camera, simply by altering the angle at which we see some everyday object, provides us with an image so unfamiliar that at first we do not recognise the object in question.)

And then there is the magic of his style. This virtuoso is past master in the art of lending an individual turn to ideas which are by no means new ... the choice of words, the placing of them, the peculiarities of his syntax.... And when he has embellished some commonplace with the graces of his personal style, we need a certain circumspection if we are not to be taken in.*

*We must not, after all, underestimate the importance of the 'individual turn of phrase'.... In fact no commonplace can pass through a mind as subtle as Gide's without being transformed, and

(It goes without saying that there's no deceit in all this. Gide is innocence itself in such matters, and has never the least intention of putting us off the track. Besides, he is the first to be taken in by what he writes; many's the time I've noticed that, even when someone tips him off, he finds it difficult to distinguish between the thoughts which are his own, and profoundly original—of which there are a great many—and the clichés about morality, religion and politics, which he has turned into Gidiana by his manner of putting them forward.)

★

I read in Wassermann's *Etzel Andergast*:

'I think that Kerkhoven had only the feeblest ca-

---

without being enriched with new matter. When Gide handles, in this way, some more or less generally accepted truth, he does more than stamp it with his personal seal; he enriches it with nuances of his own that relieve it of part of its banality; he presents it in a new light that makes it look quite different and often modifies its meaning; and above all he condenses it into a striking and stimulating formula—gives it, one might say, its final shape. The worn coin that had passed from hand to hand becomes remoulded in his grasp, and takes on the unalterable stamp of a medallion.

Perhaps that is one of the functions of the stylist. And—who knows?—perhaps we credit the great spirits of the past with having fathered thoughts that were not really their own, but which were floating in the air of their time, and needed only to be perfectly phrased in order to drift inalterably down the ages?

pacity for analysis and definition; and that this was a defect, not only of his mind, but also of his character. . . . He had few ideas; intuitions were all he really had. He never took a purely intellectual interest in any problem; but from the moment that he was absorbed by something, he gave himself to it without reservation.'

THE 'TEN DAYS' AT PONTIGNY
SEPTEMBER 1937

Gide has not held his own, this year. The young people are turning away from the old man. The less disrespectful among them still revere him, but as a museum piece. One of them, with the cynical utilitarianism of the new generation, said to me: 'We've nothing to learn from Gide.'

It's all his fault. With a few rare exceptions, he no longer tries to make people welcome: he can't be bothered to examine, or to understand, those whom circumstance has put in his path. Entirely obsessed by certain problems, he disregards everybody who cannot speak of his essential preoccupations. The most regrettable thing of all is that he has got into the absurd habit of trying to hide this indifference behind a mask of extreme solemnity; this is often quite inopportune, and it draws attention to him, disconcerts those who approach him, and makes him a figure of fun.

I made up my mind to speak to him about it, quite bluntly. It's a ridiculous oddity; and as it is fortunately quite superficial, Gide can and must rid himself of it as soon as possible.

I watched carefully, during these ten days, to see how he behaved in public. I also took note of how the others reacted to him. Some of them already accuse him of playing the pontiff. Nothing is more false, more unjust. Nobody could be less given to taking himself too seriously; his best friends know that his occasional grand airs are nothing but a disguise; that he has remained as simple and natural as ever; and as modest; and as unsure of himself. It is precisely because he is unsure of himself that he has come to camouflage, beneath an apparent solemnity, that timidity which he feels to be inappropriate to his age and position. The truth is that there are many questions on which he has nothing to say; or nothing, at any rate, that seems to him new, or striking, or particularly his own; but he is afraid of revealing this. And so he adopts this easy subterfuge; impenetrably grave, he vanishes behind a mask of solemnity; he feigns to follow what people say to him with thoughtful attention, and at the end he merely inclines his head in a slow, deep nod—as if to imply that the discussion is so profoundly important to him that he cannot enter it lightly; that the problem at issue touches the very centre of his preoccupations and gives rise, in his mind, to thoughts complicated beyond all expression.... His imitation of an occidental Buddha is despairingly funny. I hasten to say that it's not done consciously; nor is it altogether deliberate. It's simply a way of keeping clear of the debate, without offending anyone or taking the risk of saying something obvious.

For all this—and I don't think I'm mistaken—I blame his recent divagation into politics. He was dragged off to attend meetings; he was made to walk through the streets at the head of processions; he was made to take the chair at Congress after Congress, to join in the singing of revolutionary hymns, and to make speeches before thousands of comrades. One need only know Gide a very little to realise how ill at ease he must have been, when the debates grew fiery, and the mobs shouted themselves hoarse, and the arc-lights blazed, and the cameras clicked! He wanted, at any rate, to conceal his confusion and his incompetence. What sort of a disguise could he adopt? Solemnity has always come naturally to him; physically and intellectually he was made for it. Through the force of circumstance, he took to it artificially; it became a uniform which he wore on the days when he was to be on exhibition.... It was the most convenient of attitudes. Just think: imagine yourself a neophyte. The zeal of your fellow-believers has put you at the top of the bill before you are quite ready for it. But you have only to nod your head like a Chinese porcelain figure, in a silence that is pregnant with meditation, and there is no problem of politics or social organisation to which you cannot give some honourable semblance of attention.★

★

'Tiberius was more concerned that posterity should think well of him than that he should make himself estimable and agreeable in the eyes of his contemporaries.' MONTAIGNE, (II, 37)

What will make Gide's complicated personality all the more difficult to pin down is that, for a very long time, every word of his notebooks, and even of his letters, has been dominated by a single obsession: that of the judgment which posterity will pass upon him. Everything is more or less carefully weighed—even the contradictions. It's all meant to add up to a full-length por-

★This explanation amused him, and he thought it quite plausible.

(I do not think that I hid from Gide any of the notes that are published here. I did not always at once show him the pages which concerned him; but at some time or another, when the moment seemed ripe, and I felt like it, I ended by reading them aloud. Never did he give me more concentrated attention than at those times. He liked to discover what his friends thought of him—and to know that some record of their thoughts would be preserved.)

trait, not only of the man he is (and whom he has set himself to discover, to understand, and to describe quite honestly) but of the man whom he thinks he is, whom he tries to be, and whom he would like people to think he had been. Often he has no sooner accused himself of a weakness, a failing of character, or a bad action, than he succumbs to the temptation of exonerating himself by some subtle chain of argument. (Let he who has never done the same cast the first stone!)★

Anyway it is certain that never will any writer of *Confessions* have modelled his own statue with more artful sincerity, or prepared for it a solider pedestal. . . .

All of which may have, by the way, exactly the opposite result from that which he intends. If Posterity should scent, in his introspections, even a slight distortion of the truth, she might well become excessively suspicious of all that he has written about himself. (Yet this side of his work remains, in general, exceptionally truthful and perceptive.) The future historians of literature will hardly be able to distinguish, at a distance, between what is truthful and what is mere

★'I detest that fatuity of mind which believes that what is explained is also excused; I hate that vanity which finds it interesting to describe the harm that it has done, and asks to be pitied at the end of its recital, and, as it patrols with impunity among the ruins for which it is responsible, gives to self-analysis the time which should be given to repentance.' B. CONSTANT: *Adolphe*

complaisance and coquetry. It is therefore to be feared that they will trust to the rancorous testimony of those who have not known Gide well, or who have born calumnious witness; and I fear too that they may reject entirely the portrait which he offers, and substitute for it something different, largely mythical, and probably less exact.

1938

People complain that he is forgetful, changeable, and ungrateful; and that he suddenly drops those whom, for a time, he frequented with pleasure or profit. But let us be fair: it is not from caprice that he is inconstant; nor from thoughtlessness or satiety that he abandons those who were lately his friends. No friend could be more considerate, more patient, more devoted, more faithful. What is the truth, then? Why, simply that he does what we should all do, from time to time: *he reviews his treaties of alliance.*

BELLÊME: MAY 1938

Eight good days at the Tertre, with Gide. We were closer than ever to one another.

It is only a few weeks since his wife died. He bears his grief with dignity: secretly, and with no show of distress; but he says himself that it is the 'first *great* sorrow' of his life. He is like someone convalescing from an amputation, who tries patiently to come to terms with his stump. Sometimes he is tormented by what he remembers. At others he forgets that he is in mourning—and to such an extent, he tells me, that sometimes when they bring in his letters he scans them mechanically for his wife's handwriting; for she faithfully wrote to him several times each week.

He talked to me a great deal about her, and about the past, both recent and remote, which they shared. (It's with me, he tells me, that he feels freest to speak of her, and readiest to confide; and I think that this is true.) I didn't tell him so, but I was surprised to find that his grief was not darkened by any feeling of guilt. There was no sign of remorse. In fact he doesn't think he was in any way to blame, or responsible in any respect for the unhappiness, the lifelong sacrifice, of Madame Gide. He thinks: 'I was what I was. She was what she was. We both suffered bitterly, in consequence. It could not have been otherwise.'

His distress is considerably relieved by the fact that this sudden demise has spared her the ordeals of one sort and another which she would have had to endure had he died before her; it is relieved, too, by the memory of their last years together, when he was more often at her side, and of the affectionate and tranquil atmosphere which reigned when they were alone together at Cuverville. He constantly harks back to this period—describing their *têtes-à-tête*, the winter evenings by the fire, the long sessions of reading aloud, their consideration for one another, the 'unspeakable tenderness', as he calls it, of their relationship.

She left nothing in writing, no personal diaries, no message for him. Nobody will ever know just what she suffered, how much she understood, how much she suspected, what she did not want to know, what she knew in spite of herself, what she had forgiven, and what she had not. She has taken her secrets with her.

During these eight days alone together, we were practically never apart, from ten in the morning till eleven at night. We were perfectly in accord. I am sorry that I have recorded nothing of these endless conversations. But I should have had to put down every word ... And when should I have done it? I was not surfeited, when he left me at the end of each day, but I was exhausted. And he had brought me the entire manuscript of Volume XV of his Collected Works—almost wholly composed of unpublished material, which I had to read and annotate before going to sleep!

I could not risk putting down, from memory; all that he said about himself, his life, his mother, his experience of old age, our friends, the world, the future, Communism, the Church, Christ, certain peculiarities of language—and about my work, and about myself. I should need to recapture the things he said, the way he said them, his tone of voice, and the convolutions of a mind whose associations often defy analysis. It is a mind which seems to give way completely to impulse, but which in fact obeys a set of secret laws, valid for itself alone. Gide seems to be continually playing hide-and-seek with himself, and with his interlocutor. His conversation—broken into by parentheses, reminiscences, anecdotes, and bursts of delicious fooling—has the inconsequence, the unconcern, of a game; it is full of turns and returns, details touched and retouched, of pauses and hesitations, brusque advances and brusque retreats; it is a mixture of modesty and cynicism, reticence and candour, unexpected avowals and the discreetest of allusions. Sometimes as plain as a straight line, sometimes as baffling as the convolutions of a maze, it makes its way—regretfully, one might suppose—towards its final precision. That it is always aiming at this precision is clear: but it never seems in any hurry to get to it, so great is its pleasure in the long twilit pauses which culminate in that blazing moment when the whole question is resolved in a few astonishing phrases. But whether these phrases are the result of some lightning-flash of happy inspiration, or of an opportune verbal accident, or whether they are the fruit of experience, the outcome of lengthy meditation—all this, one cannot say.

But from all these hours that we spent together one memory, at any rate, emerges quite clearly: that of the deep feeling with which he spoke to me, on his last evening, of the *Minos* which he wants to write, and which might be the masterwork of his old age: a testament. It was past eleven o'clock. He had got out of his armchair and was striding about the room in a transport of enthusiasm; he looked like a seer as he paraphrased, in his own way, and with the voice of inspiration, the legends of Pasiphäe, Demeter, and Theseus; it seemed as if he could have gone on for ever.

'Ah, my dear Roger, Greek mythology is an inexhaustible mine, a treasury of eternal truth.... Like the Gospels.... And, as also happens in the Gospels, you can discover in Greek mythology an amazing number of veins that have never been explored! And such marvellous ones! Nobody seems to have any idea of them. They always pick on the same few subjects, they always limit themselves to the same few interpretations; all that is rarest and most significant they leave on one side! They don't dare to examine it.... For example: what subject could be more admirable, Roger, or more suggestive, than the meeting of Theseus and Oedipus? That tremendous encounter between the young, vainglorious, triumphant beginner, and the old, ruined, blinded, homeless founder of an Empire? But who, since the Greeks, has noticed it?'

Ramon Fernandez writes in *Itinéraire Français*:

'The originality of R.M.G. lies in his having united and harmonised in his work two literary tendencies which had not previously been found in the same books: naturalism, and the influence of Gide.'

That, I think, is an intellectual judgment (the product, moreover, of a systematic intelligence); one of those ideas which seem new and attractive (like those of Thibaudet's *Géographie Littéraire*); and which are neither quite wrong nor quite right, but purely arbitrary.

Obviously my great intimacy with Gide—with himself, his life, and his circle—has been of considerable importance for my personal development; I have always profited by it, and I am profiting still. But these advantages are general in character. The example and the company of Gide have certainly heightened my scale of values and made me more exacting about the 'quality' of a work of art. But where detail is concerned, or the idea of the novel, or the architectural (and not symphonic) conception of plot, or the choice of subjects, or technique, or methods of work, our two points of views are irreconcilable, and nothing will ever bring them nearer to one another. In speaking of the Gidian element which, according to him, may be discerned in my books, Fernandez has in mind a more immediate and a more specific influence. That is what seems to me to have little justification. Gide's criticisms, and his advice in general, are never subjective. So far from seeking to achieve a 'Gidian' domination, he forgets himself, and forgets his own inclinations, in order to see things as his visitor sees them, and to advise him as objectively as possible. (What he so enjoys, in our joint sessions of work, is just that, I think: the opportunity of getting away from himself and assuming, for a moment, the personality of someone else.) When I look back over the numberless occasions on which I have read over my manuscripts in front of him, I realise that not once did I feel between us a current of 'Gidian influence'.

It doesn't even happen through the intermediary of his work. For one thing is certain: none of his books has been, for me, one of those constant companions on whom one models oneself involuntarily, in the course of a slow and lengthy penetration. Tolstoy, yes. Tchekov, Ibsen, George Eliot, yes. And others, too. But not Gide. Not even his *Nourritures*; not even his *Journal*.

PARIS: AUGUST 1945

I had not seen Gide for three years: since he left Nice for North Africa, in the spring of 1942.

He has not aged at all. For a man in his seventy-sixth year, he is amazing. At a first glance, nothing had changed. Perhaps he was a trifle thinner, but he was still lithe, alert, restless, interested in everything; and enormously busy.... We took up our friendship, just as before, and as if we'd only separated the previous day.

But in spite of all this, and now that I've seen more of him, during these last three weeks, I have certain changes to record. The adulation of which he has been the object, at Tunis as much as at Algiers, has left its mark. He is more than ever preoccupied with himself. Having been listened to with deference for three years, by a group of admiring and much younger friends, he has lost the habit of dialogue; he has become used to developing his thoughts uninterruptedly, and in an approving silence. This has given him an hieratic self-confidence which is quite new in our relations. He is disconcerted when I interrupt, and his first impulse would even be to show a certain momentary impatience, if he did not make an effort to overcome it.

In an old man, and a great man, such a failing is doubly excusable; nevertheless I used always to be grateful to Gide for having escaped the deformations of age and fame. Fortunately they are superficial, apparent rather than real, and do not in any way affect the fundamental modesty of his character. I had abundant proof of this when I saw how simply—I might almost say how joyfully—he accepted my comments on his *Thésée*, of which he gave me a first draft to read. When it was quite serious, I liked it very much; but there were certain preciosities of style, and certain passages of a laborious pertness, and these I didn't care for at all. The irreverent mixture—pomp and cynicism, the grave and the absurd, poetical grandeur and noble feeling side by side with coarse buffoonery—all this, so stimulating and so piquant in his *Oedipe*, seemed to me artificial and rather forced in *Thésée*. Gide did not agree, but he accepted what I said with the greatest good humour.

PARIS: MAY 1947

He has never been more affectionate than he is at this moment.

Since I have been in Paris, he has learnt that I suffer from defective circulation of the blood, and have to take care of my legs; so now it is he who comes to see me. Contrary to his usual practice, he goes out after dinner, and comes and gives his three rings on my door-bell. 'I'm not disturbing you, my dear Roger? You'd say if I were, wouldn't you?' He settles himself in. I make him his herbal tea (of orange flowers). We talk away. Towards eleven o'clock he picks up the little volume of the *Aeneid* that he takes everywhere with him, and goes home to bed. I imagine him walking back, with short steps, to his rue Vaneau and stopping, as I have often seen him do, beneath a street lamp in order to decipher a passage; and then, as he continues his walk, he will think over, and mouth to himself, a possible French translation.

Yesterday he read to me the lecture which he has prepared for the occasion of his receiving an honorary Doctorate at Oxford. For all its elegance of form it displays, alas, a most obvious banality of thought. I point this out as tactfully as I can. He admits that I am right, with very good grace. But this time I regret my frankness: 'Good Heavens!' he cried. 'You're only too right, Roger! It was absurd of me to go on with that imposition. I'll telegraph to Oxford tomorrow and say that they're not to count on me ... I'll give up the Doctorate!'

I hope he'll change his mind. I imagine that, before sending the telegram, he'll read through his lecture for the last time. And as he sings out the phrases, the sheer grace of the style will give him such pleasure that he'll forget about my criticisms and give in once and for all to the temptation of the journey, the curiosity of the ceremony itself, and the amusement of dressing up in a toga and a square cap. . . .

★

★Which is exactly what happened.

People may or may not admit it at this moment, but the value of a man like Gide, the extent of his influence, and his historical importance, may be measured by the *passivity* of those who defend orthodox morality against the audacity of his ideas and the unpunished perseverance with which he has expounded them, and backed them up, and spread them throughout the world. This passivity was unexpected; and it seems to point to a lack of self-confidence in the voice of conventional disapproval. So surprising is it, in fact, that one wonders in the end if it is not the mark of a phenomenon of our times which, whether permanent or not, seems more or less general: the progressive disappearance of certain taboos and, with that, a greater tolerance in questions of sexual liberty.

In this connection, here is a significant piece of news:

Under the *official* auspices of the Royal Academy of Sweden, there appears every year a collection of essays in honour of those who have just been awarded the Nobel Prize. And the following is an extract from the volume for 1947:

'... Gide has often been accused of corrupting young people and leading them astray; the great influence which none can deny him is regarded by many as an influence for evil. That is the ancient accusation which has been laid against all the emancipators of the human spirit. Protests are superfluous, however; we need only consider the worth of those who are his real disciples. ... It is doubtless this, as much as, or more than, his literary work, which has made him well worthy of the signal honour which Sweden has just accorded him.' (*The Nobel Prizewinners of 1947*, p. 90).

THE CLINIQUE DE NICE: MAY 1949

'Only the very simple or the very great may be sure of dying in their own way. The others die in imitation.'
JEAN GUÉHENNO

He is more than eighty years old; his heart is weak, and may give in at any moment; his liver is swollen, and an abscess may be forming there; his blood is poisoned with urea. He knows all that. He knows that his heart may stop beating from one moment to the next, or that he might be carried off, after a few days of great pain, by a crisis of uremia. But of all this, he thinks, if at all, with a sort of curiosity, as if it were an unprecedented adventure: his last. ... What is much more is that Gide, who was born an insomniac, has not once closed his eyes since he took to his bed. How can he stand such an ordeal? By what terrors can this old man be haunted as he lies, for ever awake, on what seems to be his death-bed? 'By none' is the answer. He laughs when I show my anxiety: 'It's just like you to think of such things! ... I occupy my mind as best I can. I wait, I listen to the clock striking, I daydream, I recite the poems that I still know by heart ... That's how I am. I don't deserve any credit for it, my dear Roger; I just have never been afraid of *what might happen to me.* . . .'★ In the endless solitude of his nights, it is not of his own end that he thinks: it is of a passage in the Aeneid that he has just re-read for the fifth or sixth time, and in which, to his great delight, he thinks that he has just discovered one of Vergil's hidden intentions, which had hitherto escaped him. Or else he thinks of the play that he would like to adapt from the *Caves du Vatican;* or of one of the new ideas which he carries within him, and caresses, and develops, and defines, so that he may be able to put it down in his notebooks, should he ever again have the strength to write. . . .

In the morning, when I hurry into his room and am anxious to know if the fever has at last abated, and what have been the incidents of the night, he won't, at first, let me put any questions to him: what he's in a hurry to tell me is far more important, in his eyes! If I insist, and want to question the nurse, or inspect his temperature chart, he grows angry, signs to me to come

★As early as *December 20th* 1924 we read in the *Journal*: '... I think that it's a certain *sense of reality* that's lacking in me. For the fact is that I'm no longer afraid at all. . . . And yet I used to know what fear meant; as a child I was very cowardly indeed. . . .'

nearer, makes me sit right beside his bed in order to strain his breathing as little as possible, and then, in a low voice, and with many a pause, he goes over the things he has thought of in the night:

'Have you ever thought about this, Roger—for centuries men had hardly any doubts of their double nature. . . . They knew that their bodies would perish, but as for their immortal souls . . . And then, all of a sudden, they no longer feel sure! . . . All of a sudden humanity no longer believes in the immortality of the spirit! Think how important that is! It's overwhelming, Roger, isn't it? Overwhelming!'

Another day he was full of the stupidity of the higher clergy. During the night he had been looking at an anthology of Cardinal Mindzenty's writings. He was disgusted, indignant, in full rebellion—and very aggressive:

'Of course I was horror-struck by that tragic trial in Budapest. But just look at the poor Cardinal's sermons, and his pastoral letters! The banality of them! The childishness! The poverty of thought! I've never read anything—an-y-thing—like it.' His feverish face contracted, his eyes grew hard. He was struggling for breath, but he insisted on going on: 'No, no! The Churches and the Faith have really done too much harm! . . . I cannot remain indifferent to that: right to the end I shall refuse to accept it! . . . Those churches must come down off their pedestals! We've got to out-wit them! Mankind must be set free from their black magic! . . . You're too easy going, my dear Roger! Tolerance puts weapons in the Enemy's hands. If we don't fight them, we might as well give in at once: we might as well admit our defeat. . . . I, for one, am not going to give in! While there's a breath left in me I shall cry "No!" to the Churches!'

This morning, after a bad night, he was rather sorry for himself—which is rare. He made a smiling cata-logue of the infirmities, the distresses, of his sick old body, now riddled with injections.

'It's at moments like these,' I said, 'that it would be marvellously consoling to believe in one's immortal soul. . . .'

He laughed: 'No, no, not at all! In that respect nei-ther old age, nor illness, nor the nearness of death has any effect upon me. . . . I don't dream of survival at all . . . on the contrary: the farther I go, the more inac-ceptable I find the hypothesis of the Beyond . . . *in-stinctively* and *intellectually*!' Then, after a pause, 'And I think that in saying that I prove myself much more genuinely *spiritual* than the believers. . . . It's an idea I often think over. I'd like to develop it a little, if I were given the time. . . .'

(He said that, with a sort of smiling serenity, on the day after Maurice Maeterlinck had died of a heart attack, just over a mile from here, murmuring—according to the local papers—'Long live Immortality!')

It was exactly twenty past ten o'clock in the evening.

Since yesterday, I had not seen his eyelids open.

Not grief: a quiet sadness, rather.

The calm of his ending was salutary: his renunciation, his exemplary submission to the laws of Nature —these things are infectious.

We must be infinitely grateful to him for having known how to die so very *well*.

PRODUCED BY

Wilsted & Taylor Publishing Services

PRODUCTION MANAGEMENT

Christine Taylor

DESIGN & COMPOSITION

Jeff Clark

PRINTED AND BOUND BY

Thomson-Shore, Inc.